ONE SIGNAL
PUBLISHERS
———
ATRIA

IDA B.
the QUEEN

THE EXTRAORDINARY LIFE AND LEGACY OF IDA B. WELLS

MICHELLE DUSTER

and Hannah Giorgis

ONE SIGNAL
PUBLISHERS

ATRIA

New York | London | Toronto | Sydney | New Delhi

ONE SIGNAL
PUBLISHERS
ATRIA

An Imprint of Simon & Schuster, Inc.
1230 Avenue of the Americas
New York, NY 10020

First One Signal Publishers/Atria Books hardcover edition January 2021

ONE SIGNAL PUBLISHERS / ATRIA BOOKS and colophon are trademarks of
Simon & Schuster, Inc.

For information about special discounts for bulk purchases, please contact
Simon & Schuster Special Sales at 1-866-506-1949 or business@simonandschuster.com.

The Simon & Schuster Speakers Bureau can bring authors to your live event. For
more information or to book an event, contact the Simon & Schuster Speakers
Bureau at 1-866-248-3049 or visit our website at www.simonspeakers.com.

Interior design by Elizabeth Van Itallie

Manufactured in the United States of America

1 3 5 7 9 10 8 6 4 2

Library of Congress Cataloging-in-Publication Data is available on file

ISBN 978-1-9821-2981-1
ISBN 978-1-9821-2982-8 (ebook)

To all who refuse to be silent in the face of injustice. Stay strong.

CONTENTS

I.

WHO WAS IDA B. WELLS?

*There must always be a remedy for wrong
and injustice if we only know how to find it.*
—Ida B. Wells

Dangerous Negro Agitator

In the late 1910s, the Federal Bureau of Investigation updated its file that tracked a woman who'd been born into slavery in Holly Springs, Mississippi. This second report, registered the year after her FBI file was first created, came with a decisive declaration about Ida B. Wells-Barnett:

> We have on file quite a few reports from different cities, where she has addressed meetings of colored people and endeavored to impress upon them that they are a downtrodden race and that now is the time for them to demand and secure their proper position in the world. She is a very effective speaker and her influence among the colored race is well recognized.

I believe she is considered by all of the Intelligence officers as one of the most dangerous negro agitators, and it would seem that her case should be considered very carefully before she is given a passport to the Peace Conference.

The strongly worded letter worked. Ida, among several others, was denied the passport she would need to travel to an overseas conference that had been organized after the end of World War I. She believed African Americans deserved a representative at the Peace Conference in Paris, and that any written resolution should include a "racial equality clause."

Though neither President Woodrow Wilson nor the FBI agreed with her, the need for this clause seemed obvious to Ida: How could American delegates travel to France to discuss the importance of peace when their own country treated a whole race of its own citizens so poorly?

Born in 1862, Ida B. Wells-Barnett dedicated her life to exposing the hypocrisy at the core of America's vision of itself. How could the so-called land of the free be somewhere that saw the lynchings of countless Black people? How could a country that called itself a world leader be so far behind others in its treatment of women?

These were difficult questions, and Ida addressed them in multiple ways, over decades. She wrote articles that took up causes big and small; she gave speeches around the country and across the ocean over the course of her life that earned her plenty of enemies. Like many other African American activists throughout history, Ida was branded "radical" for speaking out against racism, sexism, economic exploitation, and lawlessness.

Throughout her life, Ida accomplished an awe-inspiring set of achievements. She edited and co-owned newspapers at a time when Black people, and especially Black women, faced tremendous barriers. She wrote influential articles decrying the Jim Crow laws that enforced racial segregation. She led campaigns against the everyday violence that struck terror in the hearts of Black people around the country: while living in Memphis in 1892, at the age of thirty, she urged African Americans to leave the town after a heinous killing of three Black men who'd been seized by a mob of dozens of white men. The only thing the men were guilty of was owning a successful business that economically threatened their white counterpart.

Ida was shaken by the deaths of these men, who had been her friends, and resolved to crusade against the routine horror of lynchings. She became a pioneer in what we think of now as investigative journalism, interviewing people associated with lynchings in any capacity and attempting to secure justice for victims even when police seemed disinterested in their cases. She wouldn't rest until the truths were made public: Black men, and women, were being targeted for "crimes" as minor as "being saucy to white people." Time and time again, the mobs of white people who killed them were never held accountable.

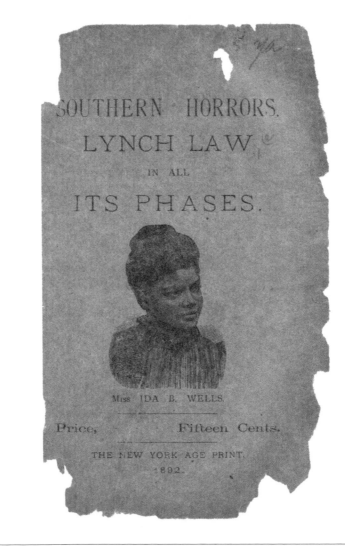

The abolitionist Frederick Douglass, whose own autobiography became a seminal antislavery text, wrote her a letter in 1892 expressing his profound appreciation of her writings. Ida used this moment to bolster the work of protecting her community, too. She published Douglass's letter in her pamphlet *Southern Horrors: Lynch Law in All Its Phases*. It read, in part:

Dear Miss Wells:

Let me give you thanks for your faithful paper on the lynch abomination now generally practiced against colored people in the South. There has been no word equal to it in convincing power. I have spoken, but my word is feeble in comparison. You give us what you know and testify from actual knowledge. You have dealt with the facts with cool, painstaking fidelity and left those naked and uncontradicted facts to speak for themselves.

Brave woman! you have done your people and mine a service which can neither be weighed nor measured. If American conscience were only half alive, if the American church and clergy were only half christianized, if American moral sensibility were not hardened by persistent infliction of outrage and crime against colored people, a scream of horror, shame and indignation would rise to Heaven wherever your pamphlet shall be read.

Ida worked alongside and often challenged the views of Douglass, as well as those of her contemporaries. Along with W. E. B. Du Bois and Mary Church Terrell, Ida was one of the founders of the National Association for the Advancement of Colored People (NAACP). Madam C. J. Walker provided support for the antilynching efforts. Ida supported Marcus Garvey with his Universal Negro Improvement Association. She also worked closely with William Monroe Trotter and his National Equal Rights League. She traveled far and wide across the United States and the United Kingdom speaking about lynching in her fight for justice.

Frederick Douglass (circa 1879). The abolitionist praised Ida B. Wells's work throughout his life, and often supported it with financial contributions and introductions to other notable activists.

Together with Josephine St. Pierre Ruffin (opposite), Mary Church Terrell (L), and Harriet Tubman (R), Ida B. Wells created a national organization to support the rights of Black women.

As a Black woman, she had to fight two battles—racism and sexism—and she did so tirelessly. After moving to New York City and then Chicago, Ida championed African American women's causes at a time when most white women excluded them from some of the considerations of the suffrage movement. Along with women such as Mary Church Terrell, Harriet Tubman, and Josephine St. Pierre Ruffin, she helped found the National Association of Colored Women (later known as the National Association of Colored Women's Clubs), creating a national network for Black women to organize for their rights. These weren't spaces where everyone always agreed—and Ida disagreed with many people throughout her life—but they provided a crucial outlet for women whose concerns weren't valued elsewhere.

Ida committed herself to bringing attention to the needs of people who didn't have power. She fought against school segregation in Chicago and championed political candidates who cared about the needs of her communities. She investigated race riots and published incontrovertible facts that other people would've preferred to ignore. She stood firm even when it was easier not to.

Though she died in 1931, Ida's impact looms large over the country's slow movements toward progress. The legacy of her journalistic work lives on beyond the specific stories she wrote during her life. It's no surprise that she was awarded a posthumous Pulitzer Prize Special Citation in 2020: the gains—and the spirit—of her writing and activism can be seen in the kinds of journalism that challenge authority and in the organizing that Black people, and especially Black women, are doing around the country.

Even the FBI couldn't stop that.

II.

WHO IDA WAS TO ME

One had better die fighting against injustice than die like a dog or a rat in a trap. —Ida B. Wells

The Picture on the Living Room Wall

I grew up on a tree-lined street with manicured lawns and flowers in a modest house on the South Side of Chicago. Within a few years of my family moving there, the neighborhood gradually transformed from a predominantly white neighborhood to a predominantly Black, middle-class neighborhood, with two-parent households of family members who worked as teachers, police officers, store clerks, factory workers, small business owners, bus drivers, and other positions in the public sector. My father, Donald, worked at the electric company, and my mother, Maxine, was an English teacher. My world consisted of my neighborhood friends, who were mostly boys.

We spent our days during the mid-1960s and early '70s playing touch football, tag, freeze, and softball. We roller-skated; skateboarded; played board games, cards, and jacks; and made up R&B songs while sitting on porches. We practiced our dance moves to Motown music, ran after the Good Humor truck, and had our own rules about sharing candy that we got from the corner store. We thought life was unfair if we didn't get to stay out as late as we wanted, and sometimes we got angry because we couldn't go around the block without permission.

I walked to my neighborhood school from kindergarten through fifth grade, with either my brother or my friend who lived around the corner. At my predominantly Black school with all Black teachers, we sang both "The Star-Spangled Banner" *and* "Lift Every Voice and Sing." There were pictures of Black people along the borders of the classrooms.

We went home for lunch every day, and there we watched cartoons on our black-and-white TV, which had fewer than ten channels and a "rabbit ear" antenna. We got a color TV when I was around ten years old. Some of my favorite shows were ones that had animals as lead characters, like *Lassie*, *Flipper*, and *Mister Ed*. There were hardly any shows that had Black characters, and the few there were lived nothing like me.

My childhood Saturdays were spent swimming at the YMCA with my two brothers, father, and grandmother. And we always had takeout food on that one day. My childhood was carefree despite the tumultuous era, fraught with assassinations of several civil rights leaders, riots that destroyed many parts of Chicago and other major cities, the Watergate scandal and the resignation of President Richard Nixon, an energy crisis, and battles about the concept of affirmative action.

Michelle Duster with her family.

I came of age during the 1970s, the years of the Black Power movement. My parents traveled to several countries in Africa, wore dashikis, and drilled a sense of pride in our heritage into us. My mother bought us Black coloring books, painted Santa Claus and the Christmas angel brown, and went on mad searches for tree ornaments that depicted Black people and culture. We had *Ebony* and *Jet* magazines throughout the house. And the *Chicago Defender* newspaper was a staple.

Once I hit sixth grade, my world became more expansive. My father was appointed to a position with Governor James R. "Jim" Thompson's cabinet and spent the weekdays in Springfield. My mother became more involved in organizations focused on racial equality in education. I sat at the table with her and helped stuff envelopes, check lists, and organize papers. Most things about my childhood seemed no different from those of everyone else around me—except that I was related to Ida B. Wells. She was my great-grandmother. My father's grandmother. And her picture was on our living room wall.

The South Side and More

As I transitioned into the tween years and transferred to a more racially diverse school, I met and made friends with people from other neighborhoods who did not look like me or come from the same background. I became fascinated with learning about other cultures and was addicted to TV shows that featured different countries. I wanted to see the world, climb pyramids, hike mountains, experience museums, explore castles, go to sidewalk cafés on cobblestone streets, and more. I daydreamed about seeing and meeting cool people all around the globe. I got pen pals in England and Norway, and our twelve-year-old selves exchanged letters, pictures, and magazine articles. At my school, I learned French and had opportunities to watch French movies and even try French food.

As I dreamed of international adventures, I became more keenly aware that people who looked like me weren't welcome in certain Chicago neighborhoods. There were boundaries that we knew were dangerous to cross. And I started to experience being treated with subtle suspicion or disdain—having store clerks follow my teenaged self while in certain stores, or having cashiers ignore me.

A huge housing community, the Ida B. Wells Homes, in a different neighborhood was named after my great-grandmother. My father would drive us past there

at times and explain the meaning of our family legacy. At that age, I didn't grasp the magnitude of the honor. All I wanted to do was hang out with my friends. My father had no firsthand memory of his grandmother, as he was born a year after she died. Two of his siblings were toddlers and the other two were not born, so the only immediate connection I had to Ida was through my grandmother Alfreda Barnett Duster and her sister, Ida Barnett.

By the time I got to high school, Ida's autobiography, which my grandmother edited and got published in 1970, had been out for several years. That was *her* thing, as far as I was concerned. I was too busy living my own life to pay close attention to what my grandmother did. I was involved in the school orchestra, track team, yearbook staff, newspaper staff, French Club; all-city band; and an all-city teenage newspaper. My world was about me and my friends.

And then reporters started coming by the house. My world started to include banquets and ceremonies where Ida was inducted into halls of fame or featured in exhibits. Buildings were named after her. People wanted to make movies or write books about her.

My father had always told us stories of his childhood, which was filled with financial struggle. He grew up during the Depression with my grandmother, who was widowed with five children to take care of. They both wanted us to be proud of our heritage, but felt no pressure to match Ida's accomplishments. We were encouraged to develop our own interests and skills. As a result, I felt slightly disconnected from all the hoopla. We were taught to have our own identities, to not speak much about our relation to Ida B. Wells because we did not do any of her work—she did. People outside of our family tied their expectations of us to Ida more than was emphasized within our own family. Ida lived her life. And I could live mine.

In my quest for adventure, I learned about an opportunity to travel to France and begged my parents to let me go. Even though we definitely had modest means, my father scraped up the money for the trip. So, at the age of sixteen, I had my first international experience and came back to Chicago almost fluent in French. It was around this time that I started to believe I was somewhat different than my peers.

While so many around me started dreaming of getting a stable nine-to-five job, getting married, having children, and buying a house, I dreamed of traveling the world. All I wanted to do was see what was outside of Chicago. And I did—as a start, I went to Dartmouth College in Hanover, New Hampshire.

A Different Path

Corporate recruiters descended upon the college campus during my senior year at Dartmouth. Many of my friends transformed themselves from sweat suit–wearing college students to suit-wearing corporate interviewees. I just couldn't do it. I knew that I did not want to work in Corporate America. I did not want to wear a suit. I did not want to sit in an office. The only problem was that I didn't know what I *did* want to do. I had met some of my travel goals by going to Mexico and several European countries and still wanted to see more of the world. All I could imagine regarding careers was that I wanted to tell stories. Create images. Make a difference in culture. And I always had been a good writer. In my indecisiveness, I graduated without a job lined up, making a deal with my parents that I would research careers and figure out something to do with my life.

I worked a temp retail job for a few months while trying to figure out my life. Then, finally I decided to go for a copywriter position in advertising. I put together what I thought was a portfolio and literally went to offices in person to find a job. Little did I know that this was setting me on the path that would be more closely aligned with that of my great-grandmother than I could imagine. She had endured incredible violence, racial injustice, death threats, and exile. All I wanted to do was be involved in creating more positive images of Black people. That didn't seem radical to me.

After working at an all-Black agency for a while, I wanted to learn more about filmmaking techniques and started taking classes. While I was in film school, the pioneering director William Greaves was making the 1989 documentary film *Ida B. Wells: A Passion for Justice* for PBS's *American Experience*. I joined his small crew in Chicago, then went on to Memphis, and ultimately to New York City to work with him. While working on the film, I visited locations that were specific to Ida's life and met scholars who were experts on her. I learned more from them than I had from my grandmother, who had passed away while I was in college. I had never bothered to ask her certain questions, and it was too late then.

Michelle Duster shortly after college.

An Unlikely Connection

By my mid-thirties, I had endured something many single women do: ten whole years of being questioned about why I wasn't married. Frustrated, I began to wonder if I was somehow more like my great-grandmother than I'd realized—and became more curious about her life. After all, she was thirty-three when she got married in 1895. She had four children and was forty-two years old when her last child, my grandmother, was born. I was intrigued by how she clearly lived her life on her own terms, in ways that were unusual compared to the women who were her contemporaries. When I read her diary to learn her inner thoughts, I realized that, in some ways, my desire to travel, have adventures, and make an impact on society seemed to be similar to

hers. I may have felt like an outlier among my friends, but it seemed I had something in common with this woman I was connected to three generations away who'd lived a whole century before me.

I was drawn to and inspired by how she refused to make herself small, even when others expected that of African American women, who were relegated to being second-class citizens in many respects. And so, after years of wrestling with the idea of "fitting in," both socially and career-wise, I accepted the fact that I was simply different than most people around me. I had been a bridesmaid more than a dozen times and still had no desire to get married. I decided to unapologetically live life on my own terms, which was a more entrepreneurial and unconventional path, just like the one my great-grandmother followed.

Carrying the Torch

During my maturation from early adulthood to my fifties, I worked in both New York City and Chicago in advertising, marketing communications, event and concert production, and film production. Always writing—for someone else. During the Great Recession of 2008, my life came to a crossroads. I was one of the millions who lost their job. In addition, the Ida B. Wells Homes had been demolished to make way for a mixed-income community. The historian Paula Giddings's biography, *Ida: A*

Sword Among Lions: Ida B. Wells and the Campaign Against Lynching, was published. I had to decide my next move.

I decided to write about my family, and edited a book of my great-grandmother's writings. On behalf of my family, I contacted Mayor Richard M. Daley and asked that the city do something to honor my great-grandmother as a woman. My argument was that she was a woman, not a building. And *she* should be remembered.

Luckily, others had the same request, and I was asked to join a committee that had already been formed. Little did I know that I was embarking on a new life path of activism. Since that time, I have advocated for the creation of a historical marker to remember the housing community and Ida. I was involved in having a major street named after her in Chicago. In her hometown of Holly Springs, Mississippi, my father and his siblings provided support to the Ida B. Wells-Barnett Museum. I decided to join them in this effort and also made never-ending requests of politicians to have signage put on Highway 78 to indicate the museum. I felt that people who were traveling to see Elvis Presley's hometown of Tupelo should at least know that Holly Springs was Ida's hometown.

My grandmother's generation is gone, and my father's generation is leaving us. I looked up one day and realized that getting these stories into the world is up to my generation and beyond. Now, my brothers, cousins, and I are the keepers of the flame, and I intend to do everything possible to make sure that my great-grandmother and other Black women who made this country what it is will have their stories told, too.

2d 322 97

The
Negro Fellowship League

MRS. IDA B. WELLS-BARNETT, PRES.

3005 State St.   Phone Calumet 6297

Chicago

Joseph P. Tumulty

Sec'y. to the President

Chicago, Ill., April 26, 1918;

President Wilson
White House

 The Negro Fellowship League calls upon you to counter-
mand Gen. Ballou's Bulletin No. 35 for 92nd Division, Camp
Funston, Kansas, enjoining officers and soldiers to refrain
from going into public places where their presence is resented because of Color. His dictum that loyal public
service is putting pleasure above general good is not ap-
plied to white soldiers, destroys all civil rights, causes
fresh discriminations, fosters race prejudice, humiliates
our race, degrades the army uniform.

 No order so vicious or undemocratic has been issued
in any armies fighting Germany. Protect American soldiers
in Democracy at home before sending them abroad in Democracy's
War.

NEGRO FELLOWSHIP LEAGUE.

Ida B. Wells-Barnett
President

ASSISTANT AND CHIEF OF STAFF
MAY -1 1918
WAR DEPARTMENT

THE ADJUTANT GENERAL'S OFFICE
RECEIVED
MAY 2 1918

Received A.G.O. MAY 2 1918

MAY 8 1918

III.

A VOICE FOR THE PEOPLE

The way to right wrongs is to turn the light of truth upon them. —Ida B. Wells

She Shall Not Be Moved

Ida B. Wells-Barnett's letter to President Woodrow Wilson protesting General Ballou's Bulletin Number 35 for the 92nd Division, Camp Funston, Kansas.

One day, Ida opened the door of the Negro Fellowship League, the organization she had started informally in 1908 with a group of her Bible study students, and saw a white man standing there. Though some white people had helped provide financial support for the project, the Negro Fellowship League most often saw Black people arrive at its doorstep. The neighborhood center opened in 1910 to provide Black migrants seeking work in Chicago a place to commune. As Ida saw it, prior to the Negro Fellowship League Reading Room and Social Center's existence, "only one social center welcomes the Negro, and that is the saloon."

The Chicago center became more than just a gathering space. Through the Negro Fellowship League, Ida and her husband, Ferdinand L. Barnett, a lawyer, helped many young Black men who were falsely accused of crimes. Many of those men were released. An average of forty-five people per day enjoyed the meeting space. Some stayed upstairs in the dormitory for less than fifty cents per night, giving them a place to rest. The reading room was open from 9 a.m. to 10 p.m. Ida and the

Bible study students kept it stocked with Chicago newspapers, so the men could look through the job ads. Southern papers such as the *New Orleans Tribune* and the *Oklahoma Eagle* were also available so that they could read about events back home.

It didn't just serve those who regularly spent time there: the center also hosted weekly lectures by a variety of prominent speakers, ranging from white reformers such as Jane Addams and Mary White Ovington to Black intellectuals such as William Monroe Trotter, Irvine Garland Penn, and the historian Carter G. Woodson.

So even when their supporters' funds dried up three years into the project, Ida and Ferdinand fought to keep the League open. First, they moved the center to smaller quarters two blocks to the south, at 3005 South State Street. The new building was just a storefront, with a rent of $35 a month (or about $1,000 in modern currency). Ida then found herself a paying job in order to earn the money to support the center.

And that's how Ida B. Wells-Barnett became Chicago's first female probation officer.

The job paid $150 a month, a little over four times the rent on the center's building. And despite the demanding schedule, she was able to juggle doing that job along with her work at the Negro Fellowship League. After working a full day at court, she went to the center until at least eight in the evening. She was willing to sacrifice her own time in order to help these young men get on their feet and successfully transition to life in the city. Being from the South, she knew where they were coming from and realized that all they needed was some support.

Ida held her probation officer post, in addition to her work at the center, for three years. All told, through sheer grit and using some of their own money, she and Ferdinand managed to keep the Negro Fellowship League open for a total of ten years, until 1920. During that time, Ida had helped find jobs for approximately a thousand men and had provided a place to stay for many others who might have otherwise been left to roam the streets.

A white man showed up at the door looking for Ida B. Wells-Barnett.

Standing in a long, embroidered dress with a high collar, her hair carefully arranged in a bun atop her head, the short, brown-skinned woman asked what exactly the man wanted. When he told her that he needed to ask about the buttons that he'd heard were being distributed from the Negro Fellowship League office, Ida walked over to a desk in the reading room and social center, which housed a library she'd grown proud of—especially for its "race literature."

She pulled out a button, then handed it to the man, a reporter from the *Herald Examiner*. Ida and her husband, Ferdinand, had made buttons to honor soldiers who had been killed by the government. The man eyed it and asked to keep the item.

Ida didn't mind giving the reporter the button—as far as she was concerned, the more people knew about their existence, the better. It didn't matter that the reporter had yet to understand why they were made in the first place. Ida could explain that. She was used to explaining.

After their exchange, the reporter did indeed leave with a button. Ida hoped that a story would be written about how the soldiers were being honored. But less than two hours after the reporter left, two different white men came to the office.

What now? Ida thought to herself. It was unusual for white people to show up at the Negro Fellowship League. After all, it was designed mostly for Black men who had migrated from the South and needed a place to stay.

One of the many ways Ida B. Wells engaged with her community was by talking to local newspapers, such as the *Herald Examiner*, about her projects.

The community space hosted lectures and readings. It was a quiet, studious area. What's more, it was located in a part of the South Side of Chicago that even some Black people were nervous to visit. What could two *other* white men possibly want here on the same day?

The men held a picture of the button that Ida had given the *Herald Examiner* reporter. They asked if she was distributing those buttons. When she said yes, they told her they were Secret Service agents who had been sent out to warn her.

"If you continue to distribute those buttons, you could be arrested," one of them said.

"On what charge?" she asked.

Ida's conversation with the reporter had certainly gone better than her exchange with the Secret Service agents. After the *Herald Examiner* journalist asked to see the buttons, Ida inquired about whether he'd heard what happened with the 3rd Battalion of the 24th Infantry. He said that he had, but he didn't get what was so upsetting about the matter.

Maybe if the reporter understood, he would agree that the buttons needed to be produced. So even knowing he was short on time, Ida proceeded to tell him: A predominantly Black army unit was sent from New Mexico to guard the construction of Camp Logan on the edge of Houston, Texas. Even though these men were expected to serve their country and fight for democracy abroad, their own country expected them to endure the humiliation of Jim Crow laws. They were met with hostility from racist white police officers, racist civilians, and laws that relegated them to second-class citizenship. The Black soldiers rode in segregated streetcars; the white workers building the camps hated their very presence.

SEGREGATION WAS NOTHING NEW

Segregation was nothing new to the majority of the soldiers posted at the camp. Many of them had been raised in the South. They knew the harsh reality of Jim Crow laws. But these men had endured training to protect and defend democracy in another country. They were wearing a uniform meant to represent their country, so they expected to be treated as full citizens of that nation. The soldiers were angered by the "Whites Only" signs they encountered; they grew upset each time someone was called a "nigger" in Houston.

These men were trained to fight. They'd undergone a strict regimen to learn how to protect their country, and that same rigorous preparation inspired them not to show a deferential attitude toward white people. Some white people considered them to be "uppity" and viewed them as a threat. The men were met with disdain, especially from white people who believed that if they treated Black soldiers with respect, then other Black people would expect the same. They couldn't fathom the existence of Black people with authority. So tensions grew between the Black troops guarding Camp Logan and the people of Houston, especially the police.

And then, on August 23, 1917, a Black soldier witnessed a white police officer, Lee Sparks, attempting to arrest a Black woman. When the soldier defended the Black woman, he was clubbed and then arrested. Corporal Charles W. Baltimore, a Black military policeman, went to find out what happened with the soldier, and an argument broke out. He, too, was beaten. Though he fled, Baltimore was later detained. Things escalated quickly. Rumors swirled. The town erupted into a frenzy. The Black soldiers stationed at Camp Logan heard that a white mob was coming to attack the camp.

Rather than wait like sitting ducks for the vigilantes, dozens of Black soldiers grabbed rifles and headed into downtown Houston against the orders of their superior officers. Over the course of two hours, total chaos ensued as soldiers, police, and local residents became embattled.

It had been a dark, rainy night when all the blood was shed. It was difficult to see anything in the mayhem. As a result, no one could identify the specific soldier who fired the shots that killed Captain J. W. Mattes. And so, in order to save themselves from persecution, seven Black soldiers later agreed to testify against the others in exchange for clemency.

Ultimately, a total of 118 enlisted Black soldiers were arrested, and sixty-three of the soldiers were charged with mutiny. In a mockery of a trial, they were represented by a single lawyer during the first court-martial that was convened. The accused were not even granted a chance to appeal. The soldiers were denied their constitutional rights to due process.

On November 28, 1917, thirteen Black soldiers were found guilty and sentenced to death, including Corporal Baltimore. Two weeks later, on December 11, they were hanged. An additional seven were hanged within weeks after that, and seven others were acquitted, while the rest were sentenced to various prison terms.

The bodies of United States soldiers, who had trained to fight for democracy abroad, were unceremoniously thrown into mass graves with each individual identified only by a number from 1 to 13. Afterward, the scaffolding from which they were hanged was burned, too. Not one white person was punished for the travesty. No civilians were ever brought to trial, and the two officers who faced court martial were released.

Ida could not help but think about the injustice of it all. Her stepson, Ferdinand Jr., was in the army. How were he and other Black soldiers supposed to defend a country where they had no rights themselves? How could the United States government execute its own soldiers?

Ida believed that people should protest the injustice that took place in Houston, but she thought nothing would happen unless her Negro Fellowship League organized it. She and her husband, Ferdinand, wanted to hold a memorial service to honor the lives of the men who died, as a small, peaceful way to protest. She

In 2017, one hundred years after the Houston riot, a marker was placed to commemorate that history.

called the pastors of several large churches and asked if any of them would allow their sanctuaries to be used for a service. Unfortunately, none of them agreed. She was disappointed—it seemed that the same churches that had urged members to join the war were not brave enough to honor the soldiers who had been murdered by the government.

The pastors seemed afraid. The climate wasn't just hostile to Black people. Various "citizens' organizations" had emerged to police whether Americans were "patriotic enough." At the time, that included Americans of German heritage because the United States was fighting Germany. German-language books were burned. German Americans were fired from their jobs en masse, despite the fact that many were fighting *for* the United States. If white Americans were persecuting other white people, many African Americans knew they could expect even worse.

Any Black church that protested the soldiers' execution in Houston could be targeted, even burned down, by these citizens' organizations, who saw themselves as guardians of patriotism. So no one wanted to support the Barnetts after the Espionage Act of June 1917. Anyone who helped the Barnetts could be said to be interfering with the conduct of the war. This was a vague charge that could be used for anything from being "disloyal" to making false or malicious statements that could hinder the military effort. Anyone found guilty could be fined thousands of dollars or endure a lengthy prison sentence.

Ida took matters into her own hands, quite literally. She created buttons reading "In Memoriam Martyred Negro Soldiers Dec. 11, 1917." She printed five hundred, then distributed them far and wide. She protested what she considered to be a "legal" lynching of Black soldiers. When she couldn't secure a space to host the memorial, she decided to sell the buttons to recoup the cost of having them made. She wanted to make sure the soldiers' deaths did not go unnoticed.

She knew the buttons were controversial, but she felt so strongly about the immorality of what had taken place in Houston that she didn't care about the backlash that was sure to come.

After all, it was 1917, and, much to Ida B.'s dismay, President Woodrow Wilson was in office. Wilson was a staunch segregationist. His administration even segregated federal employees by race where they had not before: Black and white clerks who worked for the government were forbidden from using the same bathrooms and restaurants. In fact, Ida had visited Wilson at the White House in 1913 to urge him to stop the segregation. Nothing was done. A few years later, the United States officially entered World War I and expected all citizens to show their patriotism and loyalty to the country—even Black citizens who had been denied the full rights imbued to them by the Constitution. Despite centuries of discrimination, thousands of Black men volunteered to join the fight, later joined by thousands more drafted into the army's ranks (the other branches did not accept Black enlistees at all). The war was seen by many as an opportunity to "earn" equality through service. But the battlefield provided little relief from even the most basic indignities. Black soldiers served in segregated units, watched over exclusively by white commanding officers.

Ida relayed all this to the reporter at her door. She explained that the men were soldiers for the United States Army. They were supposed to defend this country against enemies in other countries. Instead, they were killed by their own government. They didn't even have a chance to prove their case.

Even when the reporter suggested that the soldiers could have waited instead of taking up arms, Ida was resolute in her conviction. She was emphatic that even if what they had done was wrong, they had not deserved to be killed like that. She encouraged the reporter to take the button and let other people know what this country did to its own citizens. She wanted everyone to know about the crime that had been committed by the government. And it wasn't the first time this had happened.

At the age of fifty-five, she was probably tired of the chronic injustice. She had already seen too much. The lack of respect for the lives of Black people was embedded in the country's history, yet she strongly believed that these soldiers needed to be honored for their service.

When the two Secret Service agents told Ida she could be brought up on treason charges, she had a simple reply: "I understand treason to mean giving aid and comfort to the enemy in time of war. How can the distribution of this little button do that?"

The agents were unmoved. They told her that she should be grateful not to be in a country like Germany, where she would have been shot for that kind of insubordination. They demanded her assurance that she would stop distributing the buttons altogether.

Ida scoffed. She wasn't going to give up that easily. She had never been one to back down from others' intimidation. She knew the men's threats were empty and told them they ought to be very sure of their facts if they wanted to carry out their duties.

Ida B. Wells (circa 1917). She wore and distributed buttons to peacefully bring awareness to the murder of Black soldiers, but even this was viewed as a threat by the Wilson administration.

The shorter man admitted to Ida that they couldn't arrest her, but they could confiscate her buttons. When he asked where they were, noting that he'd heard she was showing them to a man as the agents arrived, Ida was nonplussed. She said the reporter must have taken the buttons with him.

The agents weren't satisfied with that answer. They asked her once more to turn over the buttons, reminding her that she had criticized the government.

Ida's response was characteristically strident: "Yes, and the government deserves to be criticized. I think it was a dastardly thing to hang those men as if they were criminals and put them in holes in the ground just as if they had been dead dogs," she said. "If it is treason for me to think and say so, then you will have to make the most of it."

When the shorter man told her that most of her people did not agree with her, she proudly announced, "I'd rather go down in history as one lone Negro who dared to tell the government that it had done a dastardly thing than to save my skin by taking back what I have said. I would consider it an honor to spend whatever years are necessary in prison as the one member of the race who protested, rather than be with all the 11,999,999 Negroes who didn't have to go to prison because they kept their mouths shut."

When the agents told her she ought to consult a lawyer, Ida was amused. Her husband was a lawyer, after all. The two had discussed this possibility as they planned together to distribute the buttons. She knew her rights. The Secret Service agents stared at her in amazement. They left without the buttons, and she was never bothered about them again.

The next day, stories were printed about the incident, spreading word far and wide about what Ida's buttons were about and where to get them. The FBI later successfully went after Ida's button printer, warning him to not make any more. Ida wore one of the buttons for many years following this incident because of the significance it held for her. Ida might have suspected then that an FBI file would be created about her in the wake of this incident, but she obviously did not care. If she did, she was right. A file was opened in early 1918.

FBI file 123754

January 2, 1918
Frank G. Clark
Chicago, Illinois
In re Mrs Ida Wells Barnett
Negro Good Fellowship League
3005 S. State Street

At Chicago

Agent called on subject together with Detective Sergeant Bush,
Chief Schuttler's office, Chicago Police Department and told her
that Department of Justice wanted her to discontinue sale of
buttons. She went into a great deal of detail concerning her right to
protest against the recent hanging of the negro soldiers, saying it
was the first time this had ever been done without an appeal to the
president. She would not give me a definite answer whether she
would stop the sale of these buttons or not and she also said she
wanted to be brought into court so that she could die for this cause
if need be. She added she would see her lawyer and obtain his
advice before she would say yes or not to our order to stop this sale.

Called on Sec. Lauterer Co., 322 W. Madison St. and they say
they made up 500 buttons and delivered them December 15th. I
warned them not to make any further deliveries of the same, and
they promised not to take any more orders. I could not locate Mrs.
Barnett today, her maid saying she went to the office and the office
knew nothing of her whereabouts.

Reported above facts to Mr. Olabaugh.

In Good Company

Ida was hardly the only crusader against injustice who attracted the harsh scrutiny of the FBI. Over the years, the agency has compiled lengthy files on some of the most well-known Black activists, along with other dissenters, including pacifists and labor organizers. Between the 1920s and the 1980s, the FBI and the Justice Department operated in tandem to continuously surveil communities and individuals who were deemed "suspect." Often, that meant people like Ida—those who witnessed discrimination and violence against their people and refused to stay silent about it. Though there were many others, a small handful of those people include:

W. E. B. DU BOIS (1868-1963)

A contemporary of Ida's, William Edward Burghardt Du Bois was an author, historian, and civil rights activist. The first African American to earn a doctorate at Harvard University, he became a professor at Atlanta University. He later led the Niagara Movement, a group that sought equal rights for African Americans. Du Bois was also concerned with the treatment of Black people around the world, and he became a leader of Pan-Africanist thought. Like Ida, he protested lynching, Jim Crow laws, and segregation. Along with hers, his writing remains some of the most influential scholarship on racism, sociology, and Black experiences in the United States.

TUSKEGEE AIRMEN

The travesty with the 1917 World War I soldiers was not the last time the government treated Black soldiers differently than white soldiers. In fact, almost thirty years later, during World War II, the soldiers who became known as the Tuskegee Airmen were held to a different standard than their white counterparts. Prior to 1940, Black people were not allowed to fly for the U.S. military. That changed after various civil rights organizations advocated for equal rights—and the Tuskegee Airmen were formed in 1941. The group of Army Air Corps men were trained to fly and maintain combat aircraft by the Tuskegee Institute in Alabama. They became pilots, navigators, bombardiers, and more. Still, they endured segregation and extreme prejudice even as they served the country they'd trained extensively to fight for. More about their efforts can be learned at the Tuskegee Airmen National Historic Site at Moton Field in Tuskegee, Alabama, which President Bill Clinton approved the creation of over fifty years later, in 1998.

A. PHILIP RANDOLPH (1889-1979)

Asa Philip Randolph was a prominent political leader who organized across the country. In 1925, he led the Brotherhood of Sleeping Car Porters, the first predominantly African American labor union in the country. In the decades after, he protested unfair labor practices, ultimately leading President Franklin D. Roosevelt to pass an executive order banning discrimination in the military and defense industries during World War II. Randolph was also the head of the March on Washington in 1963, the civil rights movement–era action where Dr. Martin Luther King Jr. delivered his famous "I Have a Dream" speech.

ELLA BAKER (1903-1986)

Ella Baker played a key role in many of the most impactful civil rights organizations of the 1900s, including the NAACP and the Student Nonviolent Coordinating Committee (which the FBI also tracked). She raised money to fight Jim Crow laws in the South, ran a voter registration campaign called the Crusade for Citizenship, and helped organize sit-ins with the student activists at Shaw University in Raleigh, North Carolina.

ADAM CLAYTON POWELL JR. (1908-1972)

Adam Clayton Powell Jr. was a Baptist minister who represented the people of Harlem, a New York City neighborhood, in the House of Representatives from 1945 until the year before his death, more than twenty-five years later. Before his congressional tenure, though, Powell fought various social ills using community-organizing strategies: for example, he organized a picket line at the 1939 New York World's Fair. Two years later, he led a bus boycott in Harlem, where, like many cities, Black people were routinely denied jobs despite being most of the passengers.

MALCOLM X (1925-1965)

El-Hajj Malik El-Shabazz (also known as Malcolm X), the American Muslim minister and human rights activist, was the subject of a ten-thousand-page FBI file because of the Nation of Islam's supposed links to communism, as well as his strident efforts to empower Black people. He was under near-constant surveillance until his assassination in 1965.

Two Very Different Fights

By the time Ida was visited by the FBI, she had already been fighting her personal battle for respect and equality for more than thirty years. It may be hard to imagine over a century later, but by the time 1913 rolled around and Ida was entrenched in the suffrage movement, women had been fighting for the right to vote for over sixty years. Even before the Civil War started in 1861, some middle- and upper-class women, mostly concentrated in the North, had started work to expand the vote to all people. Suffrage organizations came to prominence in the late 1840s, and as time went on, divisions began to emerge among white women, specifically about the prospect of including Black women in their mission.

Ida agreed that gaining the right to vote was important and deserved a fight, but she did not feel optimistic about how much change would come from white women voting. She disagreed with Susan B. Anthony and other white suffragists' belief that securing the vote for women would also bring a "womanly" influence to government, making it less corrupt and more compassionate. Ida had been around too long and endured too much complicity from white women involved in holding up white supremacy to believe that white women's votes would fix the ills of the world. As an African American woman who had faced both racism and sexism, she viewed the right to vote as a tool to address race-based oppression, as well as civil and social issues. She knew that southern white women could be expected to support their husbands' cries of white supremacy. After all, some of them were descendants of slave owners or had benefited from the institution of slavery, so they inherently viewed Black women as inferior. Thus, suffrage extended only to white women would do little to bring on much-needed racial reform.

But as women slowly gained more rights, one state at a time, Ida started to think that Susan B. Anthony was right after all: things might improve when all women won the vote. Despite the quest for the women's vote, Black women were significantly excluded from white-dominated national suffrage organizations. Locally, Ida founded the Women's Second Ward Republican Club and was a member of the Illinois Equal Suffrage Association (IESA). She worked with white women in the efforts to gain suffrage in the state. "When I saw that we were likely to have limited suffrage and the white women were working like beavers to bring it about, I made another effort to get our women interested," she wrote in her autobiography. Ida wanted to make sure that if white women got the right to vote, Black women did, too.

Two white women worked with Ida to found the first all-Black suffrage club in Illinois: Virginia Brooks, a young member of the IESA, and Belle Squire, president of the No Vote, No Tax League, an organization advocating that women who could not vote should not have to pay taxes. In January 1913, the Alpha Suffrage Club (ASC) was born.

One of the first activities of the Alpha Suffrage Club was to send Ida as president of the club to Washington, DC, to represent them in the suffrage march. It was planned to take place on March 3, 1913, just before Woodrow Wilson's inauguration as the twenty-eighth president. Ida was one of more than five thousand women from around the country who gathered in Washington, DC, to march and demand the vote. She arrived in Washington with the sixty-two-member integrated contingent of the Illinois suffragists, who promptly began going over the logistics of their walking four abreast down Pennsylvania Avenue. While they were practicing, the group was informed that the organizers wanted the Black women to march in the back of the parade in order to appease the southern suffragists.

Belle Squire and Virginia Brooks volunteered to walk by Ida's side in the segregated section of the parade. After announcing that she would not march at all if she was expected to be in the back, she pretended to consent to the offer. The meeting adjourned with a plan on how things would proceed.

The next day, as everyone was lining up for the parade, Ida could not be found. The parade commenced, and no one knew that Ida walked along the sidelines. When the Illinois delegation started to march, suddenly Ida B. emerged from the crowd to march front and center in the group of all-white marchers.

The March 5 issue of the *Chicago Tribune* ran a large photo of them, standing together, with broad suffrage sashes across their dresses. Each had a satisfied expression on her face. Ida integrated the parade without the consent of its leaders. No one was going to put her in the back—ever.

Soon after the event, the poet and suffragist Bettiola H. Fortson composed a poem titled "Queen of Our Race," celebrating Ida B. Wells-Barnett's participation in the historic march.

NATION'S WOMEN GRACE INAUGURAL

Gorgeous Gowns Lend Color and Brilliancy to Oath Taking Ceremony.

SENATE LIKE PANORAMA.

Diplomats in Court Attire Vie with Fair Sex; Galleries Packed.

[BY A STAFF CORRESPONDENT.]

Washington, D. C., March 4.—[Special.]—Feminine democracy sat bored down and gasped at the sober did its sartorial best to make the democratic ceremony a gala occasion. President Wilson and Vice President Marshall took the oath of office in a setting as gay as a garden of roses.

The failure of furs and feathers and a gorgeous array of afternoon gowns made the senate chamber a panorama of color and brightness yielding in brilliancy and decorative effect only to the scene in court attire vied with their wearers. It is certain that no inaugural robe touched off with headgear in many gorgeous hues.

Sat indeed, either, were the women of the passing administration, whose activities and a zest tinged in the social history of the Washington of the last decade. The interlopes by the score, with which President and Mrs. Taft closed their hospitalities gave an especial popularity for enrolling the future some short form the hands of the scheming ladies.

"First Families" Center of Interest.

The center of nation wide interest, the focus of the president and the vice president, led the place of honor in the assemblage of distinctive activities.

Mrs. Woodrow Wilson, to whom the inaugurate ceremony which made her husband the chief executive of the nation, wore an afternoon toilet of tan childish broadcloth and expanses of golden brown crinoline silk, a rose cast of the silk, and a small hat embellished with a sweeping plume of black shaded in bright gold at the edges.

Mrs. Marshall Wilson is becoming conscious of a purple with a freshness coat of the same material, a hat of blue crepe meshed with taupe plumes and others cascaded in tan and crinkled of fur.

Mrs. Anna Woodrow Wilson, the blonde beauty of the family wore a stunning afternoon costume of lavender childish broadcloth with trimmings of white lace and lavender silk and was the new cut taek finished with a coat of lace. Her hat of corded silk of the same shade was trimmed with shaded needle feather.

Eleanor Wilson Robed in Blue.

Miss Eleanor Wilson, whose complexion is extremely fair and whose eyes are brown, wore a costume of silk broadcloth made out a coat of silk traisame. Her hat of bright blue straw was trimmed in roses and from yellow blue crepe.

Miss Helen Woodrow Bones, President Wilson's cousin, who will serve as Mrs. Wilson's private secretary, wore a costume of dove grey Ottoman silk made with a rose coat. Her hat of hero straw was cinched with an ostrich feather of deep brown.

Mrs. George Howe, President Wilson's sister wore a sailing costume of black cassimere, a long coat of blue corded silk, and a hat of black straw trimmed with plume in tones of shaded blue and gray.

Mrs. James Cummins, President Wilson's niece, wore an afternoon costume of soft queen chinchbale, with a long coat of silk in the same tone and a hat of blue straw enriched with plumes of taupe shaded needle feather.

Diplomatic Section Brilliant.

Among the diplomats whose inimitable tie aide dazzling costumes was the British embassy. There was a constant admixture of bay and colleagues in the corridor, who posed for the first time an inaugural occasion. The countries were pitted that admixture had an air of superb importance with a chorus of pale rose carnation and a precocity carried panel of orchestria. Mrs. Marshall was the center of much commerce. She was seated her the White house looked at the departure of President Taft and the position even for the capital, wore a charming carn of black chaussierine with a tiltan coat of black medusium, a taffeta hat finished with plumes and brown shoes behind the blue.

Mrs. Bayan Taft wore a coat suit of blue crepe, a close fitting hat of black velvet, and wore live furs.

HERE IS WHAT WILSON KISSED IN TAKING OATH OF OFFICE.

President's Lips Touch One Hundred and Nineteenth Psalm as He Swears to Uphold Constitution.

Washington, D. C., March 4.—When the new president swore to uphold and defend the constitution, he stooped and kissed the open Bible held in the hands of James B. Mabel, deputy clerk of the Supreme court. His lips touched the page, turned to at random, and fell upon the 119th Psalm. So in their verses following, the verses beginning with the forty-first, explains:

—Let thy mercies come also unto me, O Lord, even thy salvation, according to thy word;

—So shall I have wherewith to answer him that reproacheth me: for I trust in thy word.

—And take not the word of truth utterly out of my mouth; for I have hoped in thy judgments.

—So shall I keep thy law continually forever and ever.

—And I will walk at liberty: for I seek thy precepts.

—I will speak of thy testimonies also before kings and will not be ashamed.

—And I will delight myself in thy commandments which I have loved.

—My hands also will I lift up unto thy commandments which I have loved, and I will meditate in thy statutes.

President Marion kissed the twelfth verse of the 119th Psalm: "They compassed me about like bees; they are quenched as the fire of thorns; for in the name of the Lord I will destroy them.

Cleveland on his first inauguration day kissed a verse of Psalms. In this, O Lord, do I put my trust; let me never be ashamed; deliver me in thy righteousness. How down thine ear to me; deliver me speedily; be thou my strong rock, for an house of defence to save me.

Harrison kissed the 121st Psalm, first and second verses. "I will lift up mine eyes unto the hills, from whence cometh my help.

Illinois Women Participants in Suffrage Parade; This State Was Well Represented in Washington.

[Photographed for "The Tribune" Monday afternoon.]

Forming in Line Near Capitol.

Left to right: Virginia Brooks, Ida Belle Squire, Mrs. Ida Wells Barnett.

The suffragettes from Illinois had embarrassing features regarding the presence of a negro woman—Mrs. Ida Wells-B—in their ranks during the Monday parade. Mrs. Belle Squire and Miss Virginia Brooks took it in hand, as did the others, and the photograph shows the proud grouped together.

WOMEN WILL PARADE HERE

National Suffrage Pageant Will Surpass One in Washington.

CHICAGO THE CHOSEN CITY.

Marchers from Every State to Participate in Demonstration.

[BY A STAFF CORRESPONDENT.]

Washington, D. C., March 4.—[Special.]—Illinois is to have a great national suffrage parade in Chicago. This is the general verdict of the enthusiastic participants of the Illinois delegation to the Washington parade.

Great effort was made to keep the plans from the newspapers, but despite the most rigid care it came out at the conference held by Mrs. Grace Wilbur Trout, president of the Illinois Equal Suffrage association, in honor of Mrs. George F. Weiss, the official parade chairman, and other members of the parade committee.

It developed during the luncheon that Mrs. Trout had appointed a special committee to study the parade organization on the spot. Mrs. Virginia Brooks and Ida Wells were aware of Illinois' ambition to have a parade which will outrival the one visit and plans here recently, but the idea was to keep the details under the members of the delegation, who received the proposition with enthusiasm.

More committees of investigation of parade organization methods were appointed.

Mrs. Weiss is to go to New York tomorrow to consult with the members of the national suffrage board and the women who have had the management of the New York parade.

Object Lesson for Men.

A more dignified parade will the idea of the march down up the Michigan avenue will arouse the people from coast to coast, said Mrs. Wells. "It will awaken our legislators to the ever increasing strength of suffrage sentiment and bring home to them forcibly the mighty significance of the woman's movement.

"With an experience gained here in Washington and the tremendous force and energy of our Illinois women, the Chicago parade will be the finest spectacle ever witnessed in the United States."

MARK INAUGURAL IN CHICAGO.

Pupils of Most of Public Schools Hear Short Talks on Ceremony and Meaning.

Pupils of most of the Chicago public schools yesterday listened to the simultaneous celebration of both the house and the senate talks to intrigue and teachers on the inauguration ceremony and its significance.

On the board of trade and in many of the downtown states there were the requests to commemorate beginning at 11 o'clock. Of these eastern time, in recognition of the passing of the old administration and the dawn of the new one. Factory whistles and bells cheered for five minutes.

Patriotic organizations held meetings, among them the American Flag Day association of the Great Northern hotel.

Huerta Congratulates Wilson.

MEXICO CITY, March 4.—President Victoriano Huerta telegraphed felicitations to President Wilson.

CAUCUS FOR BOTH HOUSES

Democrats to Organize for Session in Meetings Tonight.

KERN WILL BE LEADER.

Indianian to Succeed Martin as Chief in the Upper Chamber.

[BY A STAFF CORRESPONDENT.]

Washington, D. C., March 4.—[Special.]—Democrats of both the house and the senate will hold caucus tonight at 8.

At the house caucus members of the ways and means committee for the fifty-third congress will be elected before any other matters are taken up. That, if agreeable to a majority, the election of the speaker of the house and of various house officials will follow. If not, the ways and means committee will be instructed to report to a later caucus the program which will include the things upon which the power and influence of Tammany, it may be of the Democrats have a great pledge to fight for a fair distribution of committee places and to see that all committees are organized with progressives in control.

Kern to Succeed Martin.

At the senate various Senator Kern of Indiana will be unanimously chosen chairman of the caucus to succeed Senator Martin of Virginia. Joseph Wilson, brother of the president, will be elected secretary of the senate. Kern will as one of the senate also probably will be chosen.

Senator Kern is afflicted with the progressive wing of the party and his election as caucus chairman likely will precede a certain program which will include the doing away with the power and influence of tammany. A majority of the Democrats have signed a pledge to fight for a fair distribution of committee places and to see that all committees are organized with progressives in control.

No Contest Against Clark.

In the house caucus Speaker Clark, Clerk Trimble of Kentucky, Postmaster Doorkeeper of Georgia, and Doorkeeper Stewart of Virginia will be reflected without a contest. Charles F. Riddell of Indiana, sergeant-at-arms, is not a candidate for reelection. Robert B. Gordon of Ohio and William H. Russ of Buffalo seem former competitors, are said candidates for his place.

Kern has the full strength of Tammany, and some of the old Tammany Democrats from the south behind him.

Savings

deposited in the First Trust and Savings Bank on or before March 6th are allowed interest from the first of March

James B. Forgan, President
Emile K. Boisot, Vice-Pres.

Northwest Corner Monroe and Dearborn Sts.

Capital and Surplus $7,500,000.

M'COMBS FOR ENVOY'S POST

National Democratic Chairman to Be Ambassador to France.

CAMPAIGN WORK REWARD.

Party Chiefs Meet in Washington Today to Map Out Future Plans.

[BY A STAFF CORRESPONDENT.]

Washington, D. C., March 4.—[Special.]—William McCombs, chairman of the Democratic national committee, will be ambassador of the United States to France.

By this appointment President Wilson has sought to reward Mr. McCombs for the work he did both during the preconvention and the election campaign.

Mr. McCombs will retain the office of chairman of the Democratic national committee for a time, but he must relinquish it eventually and he has no pull in the job to his own country.

It was reported some time ago that Mr. McCombs had declined a cabinet portfolio. Whether this is true or not cannot be ascertained at this time, but it is a fact that Mr. McCombs and William G. McAdoo cannot be secretary of the treasury were not on good terms during the campaign.

Must Choose New Chairman.

With Mr. McCombs to go abroad, it will be necessary for the committee to select as his successor a man satisfactory to Mr. Wilson. As Mr. McAdoo, vice chairman of the national committee, must retire because of his acceptance of the secretaryship of the treasury it will be necessary also to name a man in his place. The vice chairman to be elected tomorrow will act as chairman and probably eventually will succeed Mr. McCombs.

Committee to Meet Today.

With McCombs' retirement expected, there will be a clear way for the meeting of the committee tomorrow. President Wilson will receive the committee and express his appreciation of the work it did in the launch preceding the election of November last.

The most important action to be taken will be the establishment of headquarters in Washington with a view to prepare for the next presidential campaign. The necessity for such headquarters has been forced by the policy of the Progressive party in opening offices in this city.

Mr. McCombs said tonight he expects much of the question of the senator will be taken up with discussion of ways and means to continue the work of the committee in the interim and thus the democratic organization throughout the country may be made more cohesive.

THE DAY IN CONGRESS.

SENATE.

Convened at 9:30 a. m.—Confirmed nominations report on Indian appropriation bill and adjourned.

HOUSE.

Convened at 12 o'clock—Adopted resolution only and adjourned.

CAPITAL POLICE FACE AN INQUIRY

Senate May Demand Explanation of Inactivity During Suffrage Parade.

JAMES R. MANN ASSAILED.

Women Angered Over His Remark That They Should Have Stayed at Home.

[BY A STAFF CORRESPONDENT.]

Washington, D. C., March 4.—[Special.]—There will be a congressional investigation of Washington's police scandal if the incidents of the suffrage parade which attended the women as they marched in the parade yesterday can bring it about.

Senator Nelson of Minnesota introduced in the senate last night a resolution calling on the District of Columbia commissioners to explain why they did not comply with the congressional resolution directing the superintendent of police to prevent interference with the parade procession.

The resolution was adopted without opposition and the commissioners will be compelled to submit their explanation to the senate.

Activities of Police Change.

Complaints of the riots that marked the suffrage parade with the absolute order that prevailed along the line of the inaugural procession today has stirred the women and brought fresh talents to greater wrath.

Every taxicab has read the observation that the police could preserve order when they wanted to, and they evidently had their disturbances not to prevent, but suffrage attempts to break up the demonstration.

There was a caution in the house last night over the scandal. Representatives Helgesen and Cooper forcefully called attention to the fact that the police had ignored the congressional orders regarding the parade.

To their remarks on behalf of the women Representative Mann of Chicago replied:

"They ought to have been at home."

By that remark Mr. Mann stirred up a hornet's nest among Illinois suffragists and at a special indignation the chip of its delegation of paraders tonight the chip was launched in the New Willard hotel the resolution adopted.

Resolved, That the Illinois delegation register a formal protest with the Legislative Voters' League of Illinois against Representative Mann in the office which he has in approving the bill for the adoption of our on the line of march paid after ? undeclinable points upon his lack of police protection in circumstances making that the women should stay at home.

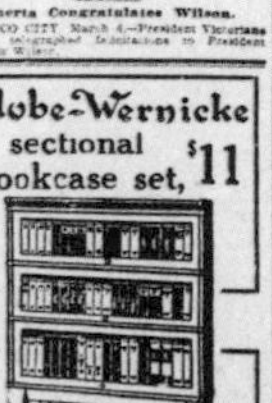

Mann an "Unmanly Man."

"Representative Mann has won a new title," said Mrs. Grace Wilbur Trout, commander in chief of the Illinois delegation. "He will go down in history as an unmanly man. Never before in the history of progressive woman enthusiasm has so brutal an assault been made on the efforts of women to get their rights."

Miss Virginia Brooks of West Hammond, who marched in the parade with Mrs. Ida Wells Barnett, said:

"James R. Mann was beneath the temperatures of the state of Illinois. Intent has added insult to injury and his attitude is a disgrace to the high type of manhood he is found to state."

Side by side with the whites she walked,

Step after step the southerners balked,

But Illinois, fond of order and grace,

Stuck to the black Queen of our race.

'Tis true, they're able at this age to bar,

But justice will soon send the doors ajar

And sit the black and white face to face

There will be seen the Queen of our race.

Page after page in history you'll read

Of one who was ready and able to lead,

Who set the nation on fire with her pace

And the Heroine will be the Queen of our race.

Unlike the Women's Second Ward Republican Club, the ASC was nonpartisan and focused on mobilizing Black women throughout the city of Chicago. The club met at the Negro Fellowship League every Wednesday night. Even though she was a busy mother of four, the fifty-one-year-old Ida B. simply could not sit still. She began a newsletter for the organization called the *Alpha Suffrage Record*, which she edited

REPUBLICANS VS. DEMOCRATS

Among African Americans, for almost one hundred years after the Civil War, the Republican Party was considered the more "progressive" party, as it was the party of Abraham Lincoln, who was credited with ending slavery. The Democratic Party was more associated with the oppression of Black people.

After the "Southern Strategy" to win over conservative Republicans was implemented in the 1960s, the focus of the political parties became almost the opposite of what they had been. That led to the more familiar views of the political parties that we see today.

in addition to the *Fellowship Herald* newspaper as she continued to write articles about lynching and segregation. She also ran the Negro Fellowship League, held a full-time job as a probation officer, and attended a dizzying number of meetings. There was always a battle to fight and an injustice to address.

In June 1913, the state of Illinois passed a new law that granted women limited suffrage in the state. Under this law, which was the result of lobbying by national and local suffrage organizations and clubs, women were allowed to vote for presidential candidates and local officers. They were not, however, allowed to vote for governor, members of Congress, or state representatives. Soon after the bill was passed in Illinois, suffragists and their daughters marched in a big downtown Chicago parade. Wearing a white dress with a white banner across it that read ALPHA SUFFRAGE, Ida's nine-year-old daughter Alfreda marched down Michigan Avenue alongside her.

See You in Court

The suffrage march in Washington, DC, wasn't the first time someone had tried to relegate Ida to a lesser placement. Ida had fought a historic battle in the state of Tennessee almost thirty years earlier. In 1881, the state of Tennessee passed a Jim Crow law specifying that Black and white train passengers ride in separate cars. Ida defied this law and continued to ride to and from the school where she taught in what was called the "ladies' coach."

Segregation was enforced sporadically at the time, and Ida rode largely undisturbed for more than two years. That changed on September 15, 1883. Ida rode aboard a train going from Memphis to Woodstock when she was asked to move to the colored car instead of the ladies' car. Ida felt that was a ridiculous request, as she had purchased a first-class ticket and was riding the train just as she had been doing for years. She decided not to comply.

The conductor tried to drag the twenty-one-year-old Ida from her seat. She wasn't going to let that happen so easily: as he grabbed her, Ida bit his hand. The angry conductor let go, but he wasn't finished with her. He went to get two more men to help him remove the petite Ida, who stood no more than five feet tall. As she waged a fierce fight, the other passengers looked on as if the situation were entertainment and actually cheered once she gave up and allowed herself to be removed.

Rather than go into the colored car, Ida exited the train. Her clothes had been torn, and she had been bruised in several places. She knew her father would be proud of how she refused to accept humiliation without a fight. She held back tears as she stood on the side of the railroad tracks, thinking about how no white woman would ever be treated in such a disrespectful and violent way. She was an educated, professional woman who had paid her fare, yet she had been accosted simply because she was a Black woman.

Since she still needed to commute back and forth between Memphis and Woodstock in order to get to her teaching job, she continued riding in the ladies' car for months. On May 4, 1884, Ida was reading a newspaper in the ladies' coach when a conductor once more ordered her to move to the "colored" train car. This time she decided to get off the train and immediately visit a lawyer to file a lawsuit against the Chesapeake, Ohio and Southwestern Railroad. The laws of the time stated that segregated accommodations would be permitted as long as they were separate and equal. Since the colored car doubled as a smoking car where white men were free to smoke and disrespect Black women, she challenged on the grounds that the accommodations were unequal. In addition, she found it particularly insulting that a Black woman who was taking care of white children could ride in the ladies' car, but she as an educated, professional, adult woman could not.

Ida later wrote about the incident's larger context in *The Reason Why the Colored American Is Not in the World's Columbian Exposition: The Afro-American's Contribution to Columbian Literature*, a text that also included writings from Frederick Douglass, journalist and religious leader Irvine Garland Penn, and her future husband, Ferdinand L. Barnett: "White men pass through these 'colored cars' and ride in them whenever they feel inclined to do so, but no colored woman however refined, well-educated or well-dressed may ride in the ladies, or first-class coach, in any of these states unless she is a nurse-maid traveling with a white child."

She knew she wasn't alone in facing the wrath of white people who believed her to be a second-class citizen, so she decided to fight back once more. This time there was no

AN ACT TO INCORPORATE THE CHESAPEAKE, OHIO AND SOUTHWESTERN RAILROAD COMPANY.

WHEREAS, By an act of the General Assembly of the Commonwealth of Kentucky, approved March 25, 1878, it was enacted "that any corporation that may be organized in the name of the Memphis, Paducah and Northern Railroad Company under, and according to, the law of the State of Tennessee, to own, operate, maintain and complete the railroad now known as the Paducah and Memphis Railroad, pursuant to the terms of the contract recited in the preamble" of said act, (which said railroad was the road, theretofore, belonging to the Paducah and Memphis Railroad Company, a corporation created and existing by virtue of a consolidation of the Paducah and Gulf Railroad Company chartered by the laws of Kentucky, and the Mississippi River Railroad Company chartered by the laws of Tennessee, and extending or intended to extend, when completed, from Paducah, in Kentucky, to Memphis, in Tennessee), "shall be, also, a corporation of and in this Commonwealth, with power to purchase, hold, sell, lease, and convey real estate and personal estate so far as the same may be necessary for the purposes of the Corporation; shall have perpetual succession; and by said corporate name may sue and be sued, contract, and be contracted with, have and use a common seal, and alter and renew the same at pleasure;"

AND, A corporation was organized in the name of the Memphis, Paducah and Northern Railroad Company under, and according to, the laws of Tennessee, to own, operate, maintain and complete said railroad according to the tenor of the said last-named act, and said corporation was, under said act of the Kentucky Legislature, organized and became a corporation in this State, owning and operating said railroad in its entire length from Paducah to Memphis so far as constructed;

AND, WHEREAS, Said corporation was by its said charter, as granted by this State, authorized to borrow money and to issue bonds secured by mortgage, or mortgages, on its corporate property and franchises, and to stipulate in any such mortgage that if it should be enforced by foreclosure and sale the purchasers at such sale should be entitled to become incorporated by filing in the office of the Clerk of the McCracken County Court a declaration of their intention to become such, with a further declaration giving the names of the officers of the new corporation, the amount of capital stock and the amount of

An act to establish the Chesapeake, Ohio and Southwestern Railroad Company within the Commonwealth of Kentucky (1878). Wells sued the company after being removed from the whites-only "ladies' car." It was a success—until the Supreme Court reversed the decision.

biting, but Ida's effect was certainly felt. At twenty-two years old, Ida B. Wells decided to take on the whole company: the powerful Chesapeake, Ohio and Southwestern Railroad would have to contend with her. She hired the only Black lawyer in Memphis and sued based on the fact that the rail cars were separate and unequal.

Ida didn't realize it at the time, but the case was much bigger than her. A ruling in her favor would have set a precedent of Black people challenging Jim Crow laws. Young and naïve, she was shocked and hurt to learn that her attorney had been bought off by the railroad.

Still, Ida refused to give up. Though her first attorney sold her out, she decided to press forward with the case. She had no choice but to hire a white attorney and settled on James M. Greer. He did such a great job that on Christmas Eve 1884, the circuit court ruled that the "plaintiff [Wells] was wrongfully ejected from the defendant's [the railroad's] car" and that she be awarded five hundred dollars in damages, an amount that was equivalent to almost a year of her teacher's salary.

The next morning, on Christmas Day, Ida received one of the greatest gifts she could imagine: an article in the *Memphis Daily Avalanche* about her victory. Even though she probably smarted at the racially insulting reference to her, Ida felt a sense of satisfaction as she saw the headline:

A DARKY DAMSEL OBTAINS A VERDICT FOR DAMAGES AGAINST THE CHESAPEAKE & OHIO RAILROAD—VERDICT FOR $500

At the age of twenty-two she had taken on a powerful railroad and won. This was the first step in what would become her lifelong crusade for justice.

Unfortunately, her joy did not last long. She never could have imagined that Black people would struggle for another eighty years before Jim Crow laws were officially struck down.

Her elation was quickly squashed when a railroad attorney visited her a few days later with news that the company wanted her to back down. They threatened to appeal the case to the Tennessee Supreme Court, which insulted Ida. She refused to relent, believing that the law would be on her side.

Unfortunately, two years later on April 5, 1887, her case was overturned by the state Supreme Court. Not only did Ida never see the five hundred dollars that had been originally awarded, but she was ordered to pay two hundred dollars in court fees.

This was a stunning blow, both emotionally and financially, as she only earned around sixty dollars a month. The justices had ignored the evidence and had made their decision according to "personal prejudices" against Black people. She felt totally defeated, and the blow led to her disillusionment with the legal system. For Black people in America, there was nowhere to get justice.

On April 11, six days later, Ida wrote in her diary:

THE FIGHT CONTINUES

The push for equality continued for decades after Ida's fights. The 1960s saw an outpouring of anti-segregation demonstrations and political organizing. Among the most widely known figures from this time are the Reverend Dr. Martin Luther King Jr., whose landmark "I Have a Dream" speech was just one small part of a long, storied legacy of championing the rights of Black people and all those who face injustice in America. Rosa Parks famously refused to give up her seat for a white patron, as was demanded of Black people at the time, but she, too, dedicated years of her life to a much bigger movement—their contributions, like Ida's, weren't just snapshots or bite-sized quotes. The Black Panther activist Angela Davis continues her work to end the injustice of the criminal justice system to this day; the late U.S. representative John Lewis, who died in July 2020 while serving his seventeenth term in the House, first joined civil rights struggles nearly seven decades ago.

These are some of the most well-known figures from this time, many of whom still carry on their work. Others included Bayard Rustin, who advised Dr. King and led efforts that ultimately became the March on Washington. The Black Panther Kwame Ture, born Stokely Carmichael in Trinidad, was one of the chairmen of the Student Nonviolent Coordinating Committee (SNCC). Diane Nash, one of the most esteemed student leaders of the sit-in movement in Nashville, Tennessee, later went on to campaign for voting rights in Alabama, and her efforts helped lead to the passage of the Voting Rights Act of 1965. Fannie Lou Hamer, a Mississippi-born activist who organized the state's Freedom Summer along with SNCC, was the cofounder and vice-chair of the Freedom Democratic Party. She, too, made tremendous strides in securing suffrage for Black people around the country despite constant threats.

The Supreme Court reversed the decision of
the lower court in my behalf, last week.
Went to see Judge Greer this afternoon & he
tells me four of them cast their personal
prejudices in the scale of justice & decided
in face of all the evidence to the contrary
that the smoking car was a first class coach
for colored people as provided for by that
statue that calls for separate coaches
but first class, for the races. I felt so
disappointed, because I had hoped such great
things from my suit for my people generally.
I have firmly believed all along that the law
was on our side and would, when we appealed
to it, give us justice. I feel shorn of that
belief and utterly discouraged, and just now
if it were possible would gather my race in
my arms and fly far away with them. O God
is there no redress, no peace, no justice in
this land for us? Thou hast always fought the
battles of the weak & oppressed. Come to my
aid at this moment & teach me what to do,
for I am sorely, bitterly disappointed. Show
us the way, even as Thou led the children of
Israel out of bondage into the promised land.

This experience was a turning point in Wells's life. The decision diminished her faith in the system. She was proud that she had the audacity to stand up for herself and vowed that she would never stop seeking justice.

The Power of the Press

The people must know before they can act and there is no educator to compare with the press. —Ida B. Wells

Though the legal system had failed Ida, she would never have been content to accept injustice just because one method hadn't worked. And sure enough, another way clicked. She would use her voice to fight, through writing. Before experiencing the crushing blow of legal defeat, Ida began her foray into journalism with the *Evening Star*, the publication of her local lyceum, or literary club. Ever full of charisma, she not only wrote and edited the *Evening Star*, she also read aloud from its pages every Friday night. Ida's readings regularly packed the lyceum, including with nonmembers. One local Baptist pastor, a man named R. N. Countee, came to hear Ida read.

Although Ida only regarded writing for the newsletter as a creative outlet, her talent stood out and caught the attention of Rev. Countee. He approached her with an offer to write a weekly column for a larger publication with a broader audience—the *Living Way* newspaper. The idea excited Ida, even though the opportunity did not pay.

Ida accepted Rev. Countee's offer. Soon she began writing a column for the *Living Way*. According to our family stories, Ida had seen her name written on a document, and it looked as if the *d* was written as two letters: *o* and *l*. She liked that different name and decided to use it as a pen name to start her journalism career. "Iola" was born.

In the 1880s, it was extremely rare for a Black woman to write about racial issues. Few women of any race went into journalism. Less than five percent of journalists were women, out of those who worked for the almost two hundred Black-owned newspapers. Now Ida was one of them. Most female journalists of the time—Black and white—wrote on subjects that were considered "women's topics": book reviews, school news, fashion, home decorating, or cleaning. Aside from these narrow categories, women journalists were also relegated to writing articles about marriage and children.

But that was never going to work for Ida, and Rev. Countee knew that when he hired her. Ida had strong opinions about everything and believed she had the right to express them. Ida's primary aim was to write toward *justice*, not just *away* from racism. And so in her columns, everyone was fair game for "Iola" to criticize—Black, white, men, women, institutions, ministers, and laypeople. When she believed that

Black people who were considered leaders did nothing to help their people, she laid into them.

Iola's articles were popular and began to spread across the country. A number of Black-owned newspapers, including the *Little Rock Sun* and the *Washington Bee*, reprinted them. Several other journals asked her to write articles as well, including the *New York Freeman*, a major newspaper edited by the civil rights leader T. Thomas Fortune. Despite their immense appreciation for her writing on discrimination, most newspapers could only offer to pay her in free copies of their publication (a struggle that may be all too familiar for those who take up a similar craft today).

Her growing journalism career got a boost once she met Rev. William J. Simmons, editor of the *American Baptist*. He was visiting Memphis from Kentucky, and said he wanted to meet "the brilliant Iola" after reading and being impressed with several of her articles. He started her on the path to believing she could earn money from her passion when he offered one dollar per week for her work as a correspondent for his newspaper.

Up until that point, she was simply thrilled to be expressing herself through words. She had received rave reviews for her work from the likes of T. Thomas Fortune, who said, "If Iola were a man she would be a humming independent in politics. She has plenty of nerve and is as sharp as a steel trap."

PRINCESS OF THE PRESS

Men and women alike appreciated her work as she challenged both gender and racial roles. Ida was making a name for herself as a journalist, and to her delight was nicknamed "Princess of the Press." She enjoyed the attention, even though it came at the price of being judged and evaluated by her looks, sometimes negatively. To this day, the burden of being judged by one's appearance rather than aptitude or achievement in a professional role is one that women bear.

Even though she enjoyed and was focused on building her journalism career, she also was fashion conscious. In fact, she lusted after having pretty dresses made and obtaining hats and matching parasols. She found herself in debt at times in order to satisfy her desire for fine clothes, and paid for them in installments. In her diary, she fretted about how to obtain the nice things she desired and accounted for all of her expenditures in excruciating detail. She definitely needed to watch every penny, as she was not only taking care of herself but also financially supporting her siblings.

She also wore her hair in its natural state—usually in some updo style—for her entire life. This might not have been considered radical during her time, but in the twenty-first century, we've seen a need emerge for legislation that protects Black women's freedom to wear their hair naturally without discrimination.

In 2020, the state of California passed the CROWN Act, making it illegal for people to be punished for wearing their hair in braids, locs, twists, and other styles that had been deemed "unprofessional."

The fact that Black women are still judged and sometimes punished for their natural appearance has created an extra burden that requires enormous internal strength to overcome within American society. In recent years, though, many artists have created works that promote self-love despite these hurdles. The director Matthew A. Cherry's animated short film, *Hair Love*, took home an Oscar at the 2020 ceremony, the award a monumental win for Cherry and his team—but also for the young Black girls who watched the delightful ode to natural kinks and curls.

Ida's words didn't just reach broad audiences, though. They also helped *her* navigate a life that was growing increasingly complicated. Indeed, changing circumstances in Ida's teaching career—the one she'd known much of her adult life—were making her deeply unhappy. She knew that journalism, and its power to affect people beyond her, was what she most wanted to do.

Ida's frustrations came to a head on her twenty-fifth birthday. In a journal entry that night, she wrote:

```
This morning I stand face to face with
twenty five years of life, that ere the day
is gone will have passed by me forever.
The experiences of a quarter of a century
of life are my own, beginning with this,
```

for me, new year. Already I stand upon one fourth of the extreme limit (100 years), and have passed one third of the span of life which, according to Psalmist, is allotted to humanity. As this day's arrival enables to me to count the twenty fifth milestone, I go back over them in memory and review my life. The first ten are so far away, in the distance as to make those at the beginning indistinct; the next 5 are remembered as a kind of butterfly existence at school, and household duties at home; within the last ten I have suffered more, learned more, lost more than I ever expect to, again. In the last decade, I've only begun to live—to know life as a whole with its joys and sorrows. Today I write these lines with a heart overflowing with thankfulness to My Heavenly Father for His wonderful love & kindness; for His bountiful goodness to me, in that He has not caused me to want, & that I have always been provided with the means to make an honest livelihood. And as I rehearse these measures my soul is singing the glad refrain "Bless the Lord O my soul and all that is within me, Bless His Holy Name for all His benefits." When I turn to sum up my own accomplishments I am not so well pleased. I have not used the opportunities I had to the best advantage and find myself intellectually lacking. And accepting my regret that I am not so good a Christian as the goodness of my Father demands, there is nothing for which I lament the wasted opportunities as I do my neglect to pick up the crumbs of knowledge that were within my reach. Consequently I find myself at this age as deficient in a comprehensive knowledge as the veriest school-girl just entering the higher course. I heartily deplore the neglect. God grant I

```
may be given firmness of purpose sufficient
to essay & continue its eradication! Thou
knowest I hunger & thirst after righteousness
& knowledge. O, give me the steadiness of
purpose, the will to acquire both. Twenty-five
years old today! May another 10 years find me
increased in honesty & purity of purpose &
motive!
```

Ida spent the next few years writing articles that had a broad reach because they were reprinted in many newspapers. She became so well-known for her writing about racial discrimination that she was unanimously elected convention secretary at the 1889 meeting of the Afro-American Press Convention in Washington, DC.

There she met several renowned Black leaders, including Frederick Douglass, a formerly enslaved man who had become the nineteenth century's most famous spokesman for the rights of African Americans. He was born in Maryland around

THE UNDERGROUND RAILROAD

The Underground Railroad was a network of secret routes and safe houses run by people, both white and African American, who offered shelter and aid to enslaved people fleeing into free states and Canada. As the historian Eric Foner wrote in his book *Gateway to Freedom: The Hidden History of the Underground Railroad*, "Newspaper advertisements seeking the recapture of fugitives frequently described runaways as 'cheerful' and 'well-disposed,' as if their escapes were inexplicable. But these [same] notices inadvertently offered a record of abusive treatment—mentions of scars and other injuries that would help identify the runaway."

Though it wasn't a literal railroad, the network operated from the early- to mid-1800s, at a time when the Fugitive Slave Act of 1793 meant that officials from free states were required by law to assist slaveholders when their "property" went missing. The Underground Railroad was as risky as it was lifesaving.

THE NORTH STAR.

FREDERICK DOUGLASS, ⎱ Editors.
M. R. DELANY, ⎰

RIGHT IS OF NO SEX—TRUTH IS OF NO COLOR—GOD IS THE FATHER OF US ALL, AND ALL WE ARE BRETHREN.

WILLIAM C. NELL, Publisher.
JOHN DICK, Printer.

VOL. I. NO. 23.   ROCHESTER, N. Y., FRIDAY, JUNE 2, 1848.   WHOLE NO.—23.

Communication.

REV. JOHN LELAND.

Selections.

LETTER FROM ROGERS, JAMAICA.

Kingston, Jamaica, Feb. 29, 1848.

PROGRESS OF POETRY.

THE TELESCOPE AND MICROSCOPE.

JUDGE SO MAN BY HIS DRESS.

TO THE RESCUE.

1817 and had escaped north as a young man. Douglass was a formidable man: he published a famous and powerful autobiography, *Narrative of the Life of Frederick Douglass*; began the antislavery newspaper the *North Star*; and turned his New York home into a station on the Underground Railroad, the lifesaving network of hiding places for escaped slaves.

Ida was incredibly flattered by the encouragement of Douglass, who said he admired her, even though she was about forty-five years his junior—young enough to be his granddaughter.

Since the appetite grows for what it feeds on, the desire came to own a paper. —Ida B. Wells

Shortly after the convention, Ida was invited to become editor for the *Free Speech and Headlight*, a Black-owned newspaper in Memphis with a large circulation. The paper was created through a merger of the *Free Speech*, by Rev. Taylor Nightingale of Memphis, and the *Marion Headlight*, by J. L. Fleming from Marion, Arkansas. The two men had different strengths. Nightingale led the largest Black congregation in the state, and Fleming was an established publisher who had fled from Marion after some white bigots threatened him. But the men needed an editor, and Ida B. Wells had the skills and the following they were looking for.

Ida was ecstatic about the opportunity. The only holdup was that she wanted to be in on the business deal, too. Once she scraped up the money to buy a one-third ownership share, she became one of the few women in the country to be both editor and owner of a newspaper.

Naturally, Ida had big plans for the paper. But first things first: she thought the paper's name was too long. Now simply the *Free Speech*, Ida B.'s paper wasted no time in publishing articles and opinion pieces that caused controversy. She was direct in her criticism and exposure of the truth around her. Ida's direct and descriptive style made Mr. Fleming nervous. After all, he'd already been run out of one town. Why risk another? Rev. Nightingale grew uncomfortable with some of her pieces, too: he needed to convince many white and Black businessmen to buy advertising space in order to keep the paper running.

She was so bold and determined to expose every form of inequality that she even had the audacity to criticize the Memphis school system—her only source of full-time income. She wrote about the vast differences in pay, resources, and teaching environments between white and Black schools. As a result, she was out of a job.

She needed to decide what to do with her life. Rather than look for another job, from that day forward she worked for herself. She threw herself into working full time to grow the newspaper. She continued her newspaper work undeterred—especially in the face of a devastating loss.

As she was selling subscriptions for the *Free Speech* in Natchez, Mississippi, tragedy struck close to home in March 1892. She didn't learn about it until she returned to Memphis and was met with the distressing news that three of her friends had been lynched. Even then, she never wavered in her commitment to exposing unjust horrors, even the ones that cut deepest for her.

The Birth of an Activist

Nearly everyone around Memphis knew Thomas Moss. A diligent man, he co-owned the People's Grocery with two other men, in an area called "the Curve" because of the sharp turn the streetcar line made at that point. His partners, Calvin McDowell and Will Stewart, worked in the grocery during the day, while Tommie went there on Sundays and at night. Although the Curve was a predominantly Black neighborhood, a white grocery store owner named William Barrett had enjoyed a monopoly among the area's shoppers before the Black-owned store opened. Once the People's Grocery gave him competition, he decided to eliminate the threat to his business. Fuming, he plotted and schemed.

One day, some young boys, both Black and white, got into an argument over a game of marbles near the People's Grocery. When the argument grew into a fight, the boys' fathers were incensed. Barrett decided to stir up further trouble, claiming that the People's Grocery had caused a riot in the neighborhood. He tried to have the store's owners arrested. That didn't work, so he continued to devise a plan on how to get rid of the enterprising men. He seethed about these three Black men who owned a prospering business. On March 5, 1892, rumors spread that Barrett was concocting a way to destroy Moss, McDowell, and Stewart. Within a week, the mob would take much more from the men and from the community who loved them.

Tommie and his partners consulted a lawyer, who told them that Memphis police could not protect them because the Curve was outside the city limits. That night, the men tried to defend themselves: they had several armed men on guard in the back of the store to protect their lives and property. Determined to destroy them, Barrett lied to the Shelby County sheriff and told him that criminals were hiding in the People's Grocery. He knew that would get him the power needed to wreak havoc on the grocers.

The sheriff deputized ordinary citizens to handle the situation. Barrett and several other men stormed the People's Grocery at eleven o'clock on Saturday night. They were dressed in ordinary clothes and didn't identify themselves in any way. Thinking they were being robbed, Moss, McDowell, and Stewart defended themselves and shot at the intruders. Three of them were wounded, and the rest ran off. There was no way the grocery owners could have guessed that the men who barged into the store were "deputies." The next morning the white newspapers, as well as Memphis authorities, were already twisting the truth about what happened and painting the three model citizens as the aggressors. There was a strongly worded implication that there would be harsh consequences if any of the temporary "law officers" died.

The community was abuzz with news of the shooting, and police descended upon the Curve. Everyone in the community was treated as a suspect. Dozens of Black people were arrested. Moss, McDowell, and Stewart turned themselves in because they truly believed that the facts would prove they acted in self-defense. After all, their store had been broken into in the middle of the night by people who never identified themselves as members of law enforcement. What else were they supposed to do but defend their property?

As the day wore on, white men felt emboldened to threaten to lynch the men, who they branded as criminals. Tension filled the air and the Black community was on edge as fear about what could happen increased. In order to provide protection for the now-prisoners, the Tennessee Rifles, which was a Black militia unit—like a National Guard today—stood guard at the jail for two days until there was an announcement on Tuesday that the three men who were shot would in fact live. The Tennessee Rifles left, thinking the prisoners would be safe.

But despite the fact that no one died, the white mob decided that the three Black store owners should still be lynched because they had the audacity to shoot at white men. They needed to get rid of the "uppity" Negroes and teach all Black people a lesson. On the evening of Tuesday, March 9, a mob entered the jail (they were probably let in, as there was no sign of a break-in) and dragged Moss, McDowell, and Stewart out of their cells. They were taken by railcar about a mile north of Memphis city limits and tortured before they were killed.

McDowell's eyes were gouged out and the fingers of his right hand were shot off. Shortly before all three men were riddled with bullets, Thomas Moss begged for his life for the sake of his wife, daughter, and unborn baby. When he realized that it was hopeless, he said, "Tell my people to go west. There is no justice for them here." His last words would turn out to be a rallying cry for the Black community.

The bodies of the three dead men were left in an open field. Anticipating outrage from the African American community, a judge of the criminal court advised the sheriff to intimidate people at the Curve. They were instructed to shoot anybody who appeared to be making trouble—which really meant anybody seen.

Inflamed and ready for more killing, the mob went to the Curve looking for anyone to shoot. Everyone in the neighborhood stayed indoors to avoid a likely death. Having nothing else to do, the mob shot into the air in frustration, then headed for the People's Grocery, where they completely decimated the store of all the food, drinks, and other goods. By the time they finished, there was barely a trace of the neat store that the three Black men had once owned.

Ida knew that all three grocery store owners, men she had called friends, were upstanding citizens. They had committed no crime at all. Ida later wrote in her autobiography: "This is what opened my eyes to what lynching really was. An excuse to get rid of Negroes who were acquiring wealth and property and thus keep the race terrorized and 'keep the nigger down.'" Her grief turned into anger, and she vowed that the *Free Speech* would battle the lynchers and the people who "looked the other way." She wouldn't rest until the world knew the truth. She knew that she had the ability to make people react based on her words. And she vowed to somehow make the perpetrators pay for the deaths of her friends. And she wanted to make sure the rest of the country knew what had happened in Memphis.

Through the distribution of her newspaper, and having her story be picked up in other publications, she hoped that the truth of domestic terrorism would help put a stop to lynching. No one deserved to die because they had the wherewithal to open and run a successful business. She picked up her pen and wrote an editorial that appeared in her newspaper a few days after the murders:

> The city of Memphis has demonstrated that neither character nor standing avails the Negro if he dares to protect himself against the white man or become his rival. There is nothing we can do about the lynching now, as we are out-numbered and without arms. The white mob could help itself to ammunition without pay, but the order was rigidly enforced against the selling of guns to Negroes. There is therefore only one thing left that we can do; save our money and leave a town which will neither protest our lives and property, nor give us a fair trial in the courts, but takes us out and murders us in cold blood when accused by white persons.

The impact of the article, combined with the last dying words of Thomas Moss, resonated with the Black people who were fed up with chronic oppression and terror. Hundreds packed up, abandoned property, and left Memphis behind. There was a mass exodus that predated the Great Migration, the journey that six million Black people would take decades later. Several ministers, including R. N. Countee and Rev. W. A. Brinkley, convinced most of their congregations to leave the city. People left by train, wagon, or even on foot. Some went just across the river to Arkansas, others went to the Oklahoma Territory or as far west as California. Moss's widow, Betty, eventually left after she gave birth to their son, who she named Thomas Moss Jr. Everyone wanted to live in a place free of fear.

Ida wanted the white community to feel the consequences for the destruction of life and property. She felt that those who did and said nothing in the face of such violence against Black people were just as guilty as those who had committed the murders. Knowing that Black people had almost no rights to vote and only limited ownership of business, she urged the Memphis folks who could not leave the city to leverage their economic power. Ida encouraged them to boycott the streetcars and white-owned businesses. She had the social savvy, emotional fortitude, and skill set to make an impact on the community. With her scathing newspaper articles, she did just that. Although she ultimately faced death threats, the loss of her paper, and exile from the South, Ida knew her parents would be proud of how she used her voice to speak up against injustice and challenge a system of oppression.

IV.

HOW IDA BECAME IDA

*My good name was all I had in the world, that I was
bound to protect it from attack by those who felt they
could do so with impunity. —Ida B. Wells*

Learning Strength and Defiance in Holly Springs

Ida Bell Wells was born on July 16, 1862, the first of Elizabeth and James Wells's eventual eight children. It was a pivotal time in our country's history as the Civil War raged across the young nation, including in her birthplace of Holly Springs, Mississippi. Since her parents were enslaved, by law Ida inherited the same status—she was considered a piece of property of "the master," Spires Boling.

After Ida, Elizabeth and James "Jim" Wells had more children—Eugenia, James, George, Annie, Lily, and Stanley. Another brother, Eddie, died shortly after birth. As the oldest, Ida often had to watch over her brothers and sisters. Each Saturday night, she bathed all of them and prepared their clothes and shoes for Sunday church. Ida especially helped care for her sister Eugenia, who suffered from a childhood illness that eventually left her paralyzed. Her father worked as a handyman and carpenter for Mr. Boling, while her mother was the Bolings' cook. Ida

Holly Springs, Mississippi.—Sketched by Mr. A. Simplot.—[See Page 27.]

most likely would have also been an enslaved cook if the South had won the war.

In April 1865, when the war ended and freedom finally came, James and Elizabeth Wells were overcome with joy. Not quite three years old, Ida had little concept of the magnitude of what her parents were celebrating. Like many formerly enslaved people, they celebrated their new freedom by marrying again, this time in a legal wedding ceremony. They relished the idea that their children would never be taken away from them and sold, as Elizabeth had experienced. They also looked forward to sending their children to school, which was an opportunity that had been illegal for enslaved people.

Shortly after the war ended, various agencies, including the Freedmen's Bureau, were set up by the United States government in order to rebuild the South and help formerly enslaved people transition to freedom. In a ravaged land, people like Ida's parents were enthusiastic about their newfound rights to vote, own property, start businesses, and attend school. One school was built right in Holly Springs. Shaw

Sketches of Ida's hometown, Holly Springs, Missisisipi, circa 1863.

University (now Rust College) educated everyone who wanted to learn, from young children to the elderly. Since it had previously been illegal to learn how to read, Ida's parents and most other Black adults were not literate. So when Ida went to school, her mother went with her until she learned to read the Bible.

James continued to work in the carpentry shop of his former enslaver as a paid employee. As free people, James and Elizabeth were able to come and go as they pleased, traveling on trains for picnics and holidays, planning and making their own decisions about their future. But some former slave owners were infuriated that people whom they considered to be beneath them could now compete with them. They resented the fact that they now had to pay people for labor instead of treating them like property.

In order to do what they could to assert their idea of a superior position in society, these disenchanted people formed hate groups. Shortly after the war, organizations like the Ku Klux Klan waged terror toward Black people. They roamed through the night, burning down property, killing, and stealing. It was a dangerous time for Black people, and most incidents of harm inflicted on them went unpunished. Riots swept across the region, and hit close to home in Memphis when Ida was four years old. Dozens of people were injured, murdered, or had property destroyed during a three-day rampage.

Meanwhile, in Holly Springs Ida enjoyed a happy childhood that consisted of school, reading, and chores. She was an avid reader who read through the Bible many times, in addition to reading novels that were popular at the time. She also spent time with her grandmother Peggy, her father's mother, at her farm in Tippah County, Mississippi.

Still, Ida knew what she had been born into. Instead of reading to her children, Elizabeth told them true stories of her harrowing life under slavery. Elizabeth Wells, née Warrenton, was born in Virginia and had been beaten by her white enslavers. She described how she and two of her sisters were taken from their family in Virginia by slave traders and sold to a white family in Mississippi. She had experienced tremendous violence and cruelty. Elizabeth had lived in constant fear, unsure of what each day would bring. *When would she get the next beating? Would she be sold again?* Eventually, Elizabeth was sold to a builder named Mr. Boling, who lived in Holly Springs, Mississippi. There she worked in his house as a cook, where she met Ida's father, James Wells. Except for one sister, she never saw her parents or siblings again. All she had as family were her sister, husband, and children.

James Wells was the son of a white plantation owner, Mr. Wells, and an enslaved woman, Peggy. The plantation was in Tippah County, Mississippi, not far from Holly Springs. Since Mr. Wells's wife, Miss Polly, never had children, James had a special place in the Wells household. Mr. Wells wanted James to have carpentry skills to use on the plantation. So, unlike most enslaved people—who worked in the fields—James was given a chance to learn a trade. When James was eighteen, Mr. Wells arranged for him to apprentice with Mr. Boling in Holly Springs.

In 1870, the Fifteenth Amendment to the Constitution granted African American men the right to vote. James immediately joined other formerly enslaved men and voted. For Ida's father, making his own decisions about the future meant not only voting but also becoming involved in politics. He was especially interested in knowing about the activities of the state's lawmakers. Unfortunately, a dispute with Mr. Boling, who wanted James to vote for the slavery-supporting Democrat candidate rather than for an abolitionist Republican, resulted in James being locked out of his carpentry shop.

Far more skilled than many white people in the area, James bought a set of tools, rented a house, and started a new life for his family. His willingness to suffer consequences for doing what was right likely made an impression on young Ida. As a child, Ida learned about the slow progress Black people were making toward equal rights. Proud that Ida could read, her father encouraged her to read the newspaper to him and his friends. Little did she know that this practice in speaking would become part of her life's work. Ida also listened to the group discuss the political events of the day. Some of the news gave them hope: In some areas, Black voters outnumbered white voters. Some Black men, including friends of Ida's father, were elected to public office.

Whenever Jim went to his political meetings at night, Elizabeth paced the floor waiting for him to return home safely. There was always worry about what the Ku Klux Klan could do. Even though Ida had only a vague idea of who they were, she knew that members of this secret society terrorized Black people and the whites who supported them. Ida's mother had good reason to be worried at night when her husband was gone. When the sun set, the KKK rode throughout the

The First Vote (1867), depicting the state of Virginia's first election in which African American men were permitted to vote.

"THE FIRST VOTE."—Drawn by A. R. Waud.—[See next Page.]

countryside. They set houses on fire. They dragged people from their homes. They whipped and murdered people with impunity. No one was safe. Despite the very real threat of violence, her father continued with his political activity. Growing up in a time when close to ninety percent of formerly enslaved people were illiterate, Ida also understood the power that came from the ability to read, write, and speak clearly. And through their example, Ida's parents taught her to be courageous, to believe that she had a voice, and that she should be politically and socially engaged, even if it was dangerous.

An Abrupt End to Childhood

Ida turned sixteen on July 16, 1878. She was enjoying the summer on her grandmother Peggy's farm, which was far enough from home that news traveled slowly. She had heard that yellow fever, the deadly disease carried by mosquitos, had swept through Memphis, as well as Granada, Mississippi. But she wasn't worried about anything happening in Holly Springs. Little did she know that her entire world was going to turn upside down.

The mayor allowed people from the ravaged cities to take refuge in Holly Springs. Over two-thirds of the residents of Holly Springs had fled for safety. Ida assumed that her family members were among them. However, both parents decided to be kind and help others who were ailing.

One fall day, Ida saw some familiar faces coming to her grandmother's farm. She was expecting good news. Instead she was handed a note that read:

> **Jim and Lizzie Wells have both died of the fever. They died within 24 hours of each other. The children are all at home and the Howard Association has put a woman there to take care of them. Send word to Ida.**

Ida was stunned when she read the words. Her entire body went numb, and she could barely shed a tear. All she could think was that it couldn't be true. There was no way that both of her parents were gone, leaving seven children to fend almost for themselves. But she did not have the luxury to spend much time mourning. There was too much to do in order to try to keep her family together. At the age of sixteen, she had to be the leader of her family. She realized that she must return home to care for her brothers and sisters, who might also be ill. All she could think was how awful it must have been for them to watch their parents die. Not only that—they were all alone in the house while it happened.

Ida was determined to get back to Holly Springs, even though it was a dangerous proposition. Train conductors had died. Passenger trains weren't running. Ida was sternly warned that she herself could get sick. But that would not stop her from getting home. Despite protests from everyone, including her grandmother, Ida proclaimed that as the oldest of seven children she had to do whatever was necessary to be there for her brothers and sisters.

Adding to her heartbreak, once she arrived back home she learned that her youngest brother, Stanley, had died along with her parents. Despite her anguish, Ida had no time to mourn. With the help of a nurse, she tended to her four sick siblings. Luckily, neither she nor Eugenia fell ill. After several harrowing weeks, the epidemic finally ended later in the fall. Ida had spent time trying to come up with a plan to take care of her siblings to keep them all together. The last thing she could imagine was being separated from her siblings after they all had lost their parents. The agony her mother had always expressed about never seeing most of her family again haunted Ida. And she wanted to do everything possible to make sure she and her siblings stayed together.

Her childhood was officially over. Even though her father's friends offered to split up the children and take care of them, Ida vowed to keep everyone together. Luckily, James and Elizabeth Wells had been resourceful and frugal: James had purchased a small house and had left the children three hundred dollars. That was enough money to support them for several months while Ida prepared for a teacher's test. She lengthened her dresses and pulled her hair into a bun to make herself appear older than sixteen. After passing the test, she was assigned to a school for Black children six miles out in the country. She then took on the adult responsibility of being the breadwinner and caretaker.

Ida was able to cover all of the family's expenses with her monthly salary of twenty-five dollars. But traveling by mule on the unpaved route between her school and Holly Springs was exhausting. The slow, arduous journey took hours. So Ida arranged to live with her students' families during the week and to return home on the weekends.

Ida needed help raising her siblings, especially since she had to live away during the week. Grandmother Peggy moved from her farm into the Holly Springs house to care for the children. With her demanding schedule of teaching all week, then spending the entire weekend washing, ironing, cooking, and grading papers, Ida worked almost around the clock. She had no time for dating, socializing, or having any type of hobbies or fun. Her only pleasure was reading, which filled any spare moment she could find.

After Grandmother Peggy suffered a stroke and moved back to her farm, and Ida endured almost two more years of her grueling schedule with the help of an old friend, she was completely worn out. She had to admit to herself that she just couldn't do it all anymore. Her brothers were growing into teenagers, and her sisters still needed a lot of care. She was only eighteen years old. Finally, Ida accepted help from her aunts.

That help came at a great cost. Her mother's sister, Aunt Belle, volunteered to care for Eugenia and to put James and George to work on her Mississippi farm. Aunt Fannie, who had lost her husband in the yellow fever epidemic and was taking care of three children on her own, convinced Ida, Annie, and Lily to move into her Memphis home. Everything the Wells children had known would become a memory. And Ida knew that the possibility of all six of them living together again was remote. She had worked herself to the bone to keep everyone together, but it had finally become too much to bear. They left the only place they had ever known to live with aunts in two different states. It was the last time they ever lived together.

Once in Memphis, Ida found a teaching position in Woodstock, Tennessee, fourteen miles from the city. Her mule-riding days were over. She now traveled back and forth by train. She worked in Woodstock for a few years before securing a higher-paying position in Memphis.

During Reconstruction, southern states were strictly regulated and required to grant certain rights to Black citizens in order to rejoin the union. When Reconstruction ended in 1877, many states enthusiastically took advantage of "states' rights" and passed Jim Crow laws to resegregate everything.

Ida grew up having white teachers who were kind and generous. Her father had taught her that she needed to fight for her rights and no one could make her feel that she was less than anyone else. Ida had learned from her teachers to be responsible and

A typical rural schoolhouse in the 1880s.

Beale Street Historic District in Memphis, Tennessee, circa 1970.

to serve others. The Christian instructors encouraged Ida to act like a lady at all times, a lesson she took to heart.

Formerly enslaved women, like her mother, worked particularly hard to be lady-like. As enslaved workers, they had toiled long, hard hours doing grueling work. At the end of each day, their backs had ached and their hands had become calloused from manual labor. After the war, Black women looked forward to being treated with the same respect as white women. They cherished the opportunity to partake in otherwise commonplace practices they had been denied as enslaved persons, like caring for their own children and households and having control over their living spaces. They wanted to be shown the same level of respect that white women enjoyed. They believed that looking and acting like "ladies" were ways to obtain that respect. White gloves, fine manners, and starched curtains took on enormous meaning.

So of course, when Tennessee passed its first Jim Crow law in 1881, specifying that Black and white train passengers ride in separate cars, Ida was incensed. After all she'd learned and experienced, how could she *not* fight to remain in her rightful place as a lady?

Ida's belief that she deserved to enjoy all of the opportunities and freedoms that were the promise of the United States was a driving force in her life. She went on to fight for justice and equality in the law, education, housing, employment, and politics. And her tactic of truth-telling as a weapon to challenge unequal systems and structures has impacted our country for decades since. Countless activists, organizers, journalists, and public officials have drawn inspiration from her life and the work she did to push the country toward a freedom that many people have never known.

V.

400 YEARS OF PROGRESS

The South resented giving the Afro-American his freedom, the ballot box, and the Civil Rights Law. —Ida B. Wells

---

1619   First Africans who were enslaved arrived in British North America

---

1775   Quakers created the first antislavery society

1776   July 4 – Declaration of Independence

1808   Congress banned the external slave trade

1816   African Methodist Episcopal Church formally established by former slaves

---

1838   Frederick Douglass escaped from slavery

1850   September 18 – Fugitive slave law enacted that required that escaped slaves be returned to their owners (even if they were caught in what was technically a "free" state)

1852   February 18 – Ferdinand Lee Barnett born

1857 The *Dred Scott v. Sandford* U.S. Supreme Court decision stated that slaves were not citizens of the United States, and therefore they could not expect any protection from the federal government or courts.

1860 Abraham Lincoln elected president

1862 July 16 – Ida Bell Wells born

1863 January 1 – Emancipation Proclamation issued by President Lincoln, technically freeing only the enslaved African Americans in states that were on the South's side of the Civil War.

1865 • March 3 – Freedmen's Bureau established

• April 15 – President Lincoln assassinated

• May 9 – Civil War ended, Reconstruction started

• June 19 – Enslaved people in Texas learned they were free, which is what the Juneteenth holiday is based on

• December 6 – Thirteenth Amendment abolished slavery and involuntary servitude, except as punishment for a crime

• Ku Klux Klan formed in Tennessee

1866 Shaw University (now Rust College) established

1868 July 9 – Fourteenth Amendment granted citizenship to all who were born or naturalized in the United States

1870 February 3 – Fifteenth Amendment granted voting rights to citizens regardless of race, color, or previous servitude. This made it so formerly enslaved men could vote, but women could not.

1872	Freedmen's Bureau disbanded
1877	Reconstruction ended
1878	Ida's parents and infant brother Stanley died
1881	Jim Crow laws regarding segregation on public transportation implemented in Tennessee
1883	September 15 – Ida removed from Chesapeake, Ohio and Southwestern Railroad train on ride going from Memphis to Woodstock
1884	• May 4 – Ida removed from train going from Woodstock to Memphis. She filed lawsuit against railroad. • December 24 – Ida won lawsuit against railroad
1887	April – Ida's lawsuit overturned by Tennessee Supreme Court
1889	Ida became one-third owner of Memphis *Free Speech*
1891	Ida lost teaching job, put all energy into the newspaper
1892	• March 9 – Ida's friends Thomas Moss, Calvin McDowell, and William Stewart were killed. She wrote articles exposing the truth about lynching, lost her printing press, and was exiled from the South. • May – Ida moved to New York City, worked with T. Thomas Fortune on *New York Age*, became one-fourth co-owner • Ida published *Southern Horrors: Lynch Law in All Its Phases* • Ida started speaking at churches in New York and Philadelphia about lynching atrocities

1893 • Ida traveled on speaking tour in the United Kingdom

• Cowrote, edited, and published the pamphlet *The Reason Why the Colored American Is Not in the World's Columbian Exposition*, cowritten with Frederick Douglass, Ferdinand L. Barnett, and Irvine Garland Penn. Distributed over ten thousand copies at the World's Fair.

• Ida founded Ida B. Wells Club in Chicago

1894 Ida went on her second speaking tour in England, which lasted four months

1895 • February 20 – Frederick Douglass died

• Ida wrote and published *A Red Record: Tabulated Statistics and Alleged Causes of Lynching in the United States, 1892–1893–1894*

• June 27 – Married Ferdinand L. Barnett at Bethel AME Church. Hyphenated her name to Wells-Barnett

1896 • *Plessy v. Ferguson* U.S. Supreme Court ruling happened, which upheld the constitutionality of racial segregation laws for public facilities as long as they were equal in quality

• Ida's son Charles Aked Barnett born

• Ida cofounded National Association of Colored Women

1897 • Ida's son Herman Kohlsaat Barnett born

• Ida established first kindergarten in Chicago for Black children

1898 • February 22 – Postmaster Frazier B. Baker and his infant killed in Lake City, South Carolina

• Ida visited President William McKinley to ask him to treat lynching as a federal crime

• Spanish-American War lasted from April to August

1899   Ida wrote and published pamphlet *Lynch Law in Georgia*

1900   Ida wrote and published pamphlet *Mob Rule in New Orleans*

1901   Ida's daughter Ida Bell Barnett Jr. born

1904   Ida's daughter Alfreda Barnett born

1908   Ida started Negro Fellowship League at Grace Presbyterian Church as extension of Bible study class

1909   • Formation of NAACP in response to 1908 Springfield, Illinois, race riot

   • Lynching of Will "Frog" James in Cairo, Illinois—Ida B. met with Governor Charles S. Deneen to discuss

1910   Negro Fellowship League moved into its first space at 2830 South State Street

1913   • January 30 – Ida cofounded the Alpha Suffrage Club

   • March 3 – Ida integrated Washington, DC, suffrage march

   • June 26 – Illinois passed restricted suffrage for women

   • Negro Fellowship League moved to 3005 South State Street

   • Ida started working as probation officer

1916   Ida stopped working as probation officer

1917   • April 6 – United States entered World War I

   • July – East St. Louis, Illinois, race riot occurred

- Ida wrote and published pamphlet *The East St. Louis Massacre: The Greatest Outrage of the Century*

- August – Houston race riot involving Black soldiers at Camp Logan occured

1918
- Ida visited and investigated by FBI for passing out martyred Negro soldiers buttons

- November 11 – World War I ends

1919
- More than twenty-five race riots took place around the country, including in Elaine, Arkansas, in what was called Red Summer

- Ida investigated by FBI, passport to the Paris Peace Conference denied

1920
- Negro Fellowship League closed

- Ida wrote and published *The Arkansas Race Riot*

- Ida visited Elaine massacre prisoners in Little Rock

1929 The Great Depression started

1930 Ida ran and lost race for Illinois State Senate

1931 March 25 – Ida B. Wells died

1932 President Franklin D. Roosevelt elected and implemented New Deal in 1933, which lasted through 1939

1936 March 11 – Ferdinand L. Barnett died

1941 Ida B. Wells Homes opened in Chicago

1954 *Brown v. Board of Education* ruling came down, which desegregated schools in the United States

1955
- August 28 – Emmett Till lynched

- December 1 –Rosa Parks's refusal to give up her seat on the bus started the Montgomery bus boycott, which lasted 381 days

1963 November 22 – President John F. Kennedy assassinated

1965
- February 14 – Malcolm X assassinated

- August 6 – Voting Rights Act signed by President Lyndon B. Johnson

1968
- April 4 – Dr. Martin Luther King Jr. assassinated

- Riots across multiple cities

1970 *Crusade for Justice: The Autobiography of Ida B. Wells*, edited by Alfreda Barnett Duster, was published by the University of Chicago Press

1974 Ida B. Wells-Barnett House at 3624 S. Dr. Martin Luther King Jr. Drive given National Historic Landmark status

1985 Ida inducted into Tennessee Press Hall of Fame

1987 Tennessee Historic Commission placed Ida B. Wells commemorative marker on Beale Street in Memphis

1988
- The Ida B. Wells Memorial Foundation established by five of her grandchildren (her daughter Alfreda's children)

- Ida inducted into National Women's Hall of Fame in Seneca Falls, New York

1989	William Greaves aired his documentary film for PBS's American Experience series, *Ida B. Wells: A Passion for Justice*
1990	February 1 – United States Postal Service issued twenty-five-cent Black heritage postage stamp in honor of Ida B. Wells
1991	• Post office in Holly Springs, Mississippi, named after Ida B. Wells • Historical marker installed for People's Grocery in Memphis
1995	The Ida B. Wells-Barnett House designated Chicago landmark
1996	Ida B. Wells Family Art Gallery charted in Holly Springs, Mississippi. It was renamed the Ida B. Wells-Barnett Museum in 2002.
2002	Ida B. Wells Homes in Chicago started being demolished
2005	June – The United States Senate issued a resolution (S Res 39) apologizing for not ever passing a bill to make lynching a federal crime. Ida's great-grandson Dan Duster spoke before the body.
2008	• Paula Giddings's biography of Ida, *Ida: A Sword Among Lions: Ida B. Wells and the Campaign Against Lynching,* published • *Ida In Her Own Words*, edited by Michelle Duster, published • Ida B. Wells Commemorative Art Committee formed. Commissioned sculptor Richard Hunt in 2011 to create and install work at 37th Street and Langley Avenue as the first monument to a Black woman in Chicago • Barack Obama elected as the first African American president of the United States

2010
- *Ida From Abroad*, edited by Michelle Duster, published

- Room conamed after Ida B. Wells in United States Senate's Russell Building

2011 Ida inducted into Chicago Literary Hall of Fame

2016
- February – Ida B. Wells Society for Investigative Reporting founded

- September 24 – Smithsonian's National Museum of African American History and Culture opened, which includes significant exhibit on Ida B. Wells

2018
- March 8 – Delayed *New York Times* obituary published as part of the Overlooked series

- March 16 – *New York Times The Daily* podcast about Ida B. aired

- April 26 – Equal Justice Initiative opened two institutions in Montgomery, Alabama. The Legacy Museum: From Enslavement to Mass Incarceration, and the National Memorial for Peace and Justice, which includes quotes and images of Ida B. Wells

- July 26 – Congress Parkway in Chicago renamed Ida B. Wells Drive

2019
- February 11 – Ida B. Wells Drive street sign unveiling ceremony

- February – the United States Senate antilynching bill S. 488 (Justice for Victims of Lynching Act of 2019), introduced by Senators Cory Booker, Kamala Harris, and Tim Scott, passed the Senate on the 14th. The House antilynching bill H.R. 35, (Emmett Till Antilynching Act) introduced by Representative Bobby Rush, passed the House on the 26th. Either bill would make lynching a federal crime. Due to the House's addition of the name "Emmett Till Antilynching Act," the bill was sent back to the Senate for a vote and blocked by Senator Rand Paul since June 2020.

• March – Historical marker placed in Zion Cemetery in Memphis honoring William Stewart, Calvin McDowell, and Thomas Moss

• July 13 – Historical marker honoring Ida B. Wells placed in town square of her hometown, Holly Springs, Mississippi

• July 20 – Honorary Ida B. Wells Way and historical marker placed on 37th Street and King Drive in Chicago

• August – Ida inducted into Mississippi Writers Trail

2020   • May 4 – Ida awarded posthumous 2020 Pulitzer Prize Special Citation

• May 13 – Second edition of autobiography *Crusade for Justice: The Autobiography of Ida B. Wells* released by the University of Chicago Press

• May 30 – Statue of Edward Carmack (newspaper editor and senator who harassed Ida B. Wells) toppled by demonstrators

• June – Legislative Plaza in Nashville unofficially renamed by demonstrators as Ida B. Wells Plaza

• August 20 – Senator Kamala Harris accepts nomination for vice president and running mate to presidential candidate Joe Biden (former vice president)

• Memphis Suffrage Monument "Equality Trailblazers," which includes Ida B. Wells, created in Memphis

VI.

A POWERFUL LEGACY

They had destroyed my paper, in which every dollar I had in the world was invested. They had made me an exile and threatened my life for hinting at the truth. I felt that I owed it to myself and my race to tell the whole truth.
—Ida B. Wells

Defending and Embracing Our Authentic Selves

At just sixteen, Ida had to join the world of adults—and navigate the scrutiny and danger that greeted late-nineteenth-century women—all on her own. That meant adhering to the so-called cult of true womanhood, in which "the ideal woman was seen not only as submissive, but also gentle, innocent, pure, modest, and pious," as the historian Linda O. McMurry writes in her biography of Ida, *To Keep the Waters Troubled: The Life of Ida B. Wells*. With such strict social codes guiding her life, the teenage Ida would have taken great care to avoid slanderous rumors and protect her reputation.

Once her siblings had been nursed back to health, Ida thought about the daunting task of taking care of everyone financially. Luckily, her sister informed her that their father had trusted his doctor to keep a sum of money safe for use in the event his wife or children needed help. According to her autobiography, Ida met him one evening shortly after her parents died in 1878 to get the money. Apparently, her visit was observed by a few chatty neighbors. Rumors began to circulate that the teenaged Black girl and adult white male had met for insidious reasons. The exchange of money did not help.

The salacious lies combined with the loss of her parents caused her a great deal of pain. She felt utterly alone yet had to forge through. Decades later she wrote in her autobiography:

> Of course as a young, inexperienced girl who had never had a beau, too young to have been out in company except at children's parties, I knew nothing whatever of the world's ways of looking at things and never dreamed that the community would not understand why I didn't want our children separated. But someone said that I had been downtown inquiring for Dr. Gray shortly after I had come from the country. They heard him tell me to tell my sister he would get the money, meaning my father's money, and bring it to us that night. It was easy for that type of mind to deduce and spread the rumor that already, as young as I was, I had been heard asking white men for money and that was the reason I wanted to live there by myself with the children.

> I am quite sure that never in all my life have I suffered such a shock as I did when I heard that misconstruction that had been placed upon my determination to keep my brothers and sisters together. As I look back at it now I can perhaps understand the type of mind which drew such conclusions. And no one suggested that I was laying myself open to gossiping tongues.

RECY TAYLOR

Recy Taylor was a young mother and a sharecropper who lived in Alabama in the early 1900s. One day in 1944, when she was walking home from church in Abbeville, the segregated town she and her family called home, the twenty-four-year-old was abducted and later gang-raped by six white men. They left her on the side of the road after the brutal assault, presumably to die. Though Taylor reported the attack to the police, the men were never brought to justice—even when her case made it to trial, a jury composed entirely of white men dismissed the charges within five minutes. Taylor's case galvanized the local community and the national Black press. The NAACP, including the activist Rosa Parks, advocated for her as part of a group of concerned people who formed the Committee for Equal Justice for Mrs. Recy Taylor. Even following their efforts, though, the men responsible for raping her were never prosecuted (despite several confessing to the heinous act). More than sixty years later, a 2007 documentary about this unimaginable ordeal, called *The Rape of Recy Taylor*, detailed the case itself while following the many people who fought on her behalf and how Taylor's case exemplified the constant threat of sexual violence that Black women have contended with for centuries.

Ida B. Wells was not the first or last Black woman who needed to fend off unwarranted criticism or defend her reputation. Black women have endured being stereotyped and caricatured as hypersexual, immoral, unsophisticated, angry, and violent people. This made Ida extra vigilant in how she dressed and conducted herself. Not only to command respect as someone who would present herself in a certain way, but also to stay safe. Black women historically have had much less protection under the law than other women, starting with the omnipresent practice of rape and separation from their children that typified slavery. Victims of sexual crimes were often blamed for their trauma and almost never saw their perpetrators punished. This dynamic led to a deep silence about the violations.

From Recy Taylor, who was raped by several white men in 1944 while on her way home from church, to the string of Black women who were sexually assaulted by police in Oklahoma in 2014–15, Black women have always been especially vulnerable.

In addition to navigating physical danger, African American women had to endure having their physical characteristics vilified and viewed as a liability. Full lips, round butts, browner skin, "kinky" hair, broad noses, and other physical characteristics have been denigrated for their difference from European features. From Sarah

DANIEL HOLTZCLAW

Much more recently, in December 2015, a former Oklahoma City police officer named Daniel Holtzclaw was convicted of raping several Black women in the area. According to prosecutors, Holtzclaw began assaulting Black women in 2014, often targeting them during routine traffic stops that he made while on duty. His victims said Holtzclaw chose them because he knew they were unlikely to be believed by officers if they tried to report his crimes—all of them were Black, and many lived in one of Oklahoma City's poorest neighborhoods. They detailed horrific assaults, and at the end of Holtzclaw's trial, a jury found him guilty of many of the thirty-six charges brought against him, including four of six first-degree rape charges, one charge of second-degree rape with instrumentation, four counts of forcible sodomy, six counts of sexual battery, and three procuring lewd exhibition charges. Holtzclaw, who was sentenced to 263 years in prison in 2016, was denied an appeal in 2019.

Baartman being paraded around like a circus freak show in the 1800s to the tennis champion Serena Williams being referred to in masculine terms, Black women have been attacked for their appearances.

Ida was aware of the difference in protection she could expect compared to white women, and she did everything possible to avoid dangerous situations or others that could tarnish her reputation. She was so vigilant about it that she demanded that a pastor write a letter to speak to her character in 1891 after hearing that he had been disparaging her name in his community. Ida had stayed over as a guest of the minister and his wife while in Vicksburg, Mississippi, on a sales trip for the *Free Speech*. Both Ida and the sister-in-law of the minister stayed at the house. The two women happened to converse with some men who visited the house during their stay.

Later, Ida learned that the pastor had spoken to people about how virtuous northern women were in comparison to southern women, implying that the southern-born Ida was herself not virtuous. The minister's wife had fished Ida's torn-up mail out of the trash and read a letter in which Ida referenced losing her teaching position in Memphis. After his wife relayed the contents of Ida's private correspondence, the minister twisted whatever Ida had said in her letter to imply that her lack of virtue, versus her outspokenness, explained why the Memphis school system had not renewed Ida's contract to teach. Not only did he and his wife sully Ida's name, they also

LOVE and BEAUTY--SARTJEE the HOTTENTOT VENUS.

Dubd October 1811 by Charlton Coopen Pimlico

N.B. She was the first female ever came over to this Country & was exhibited at Mr Bigley's Rooms in Spring Gardens Cockspur St

SARAH BAARTMAN

Sarah Baartman, sometimes known as Saartje Baartman, was born in 1789 in what is now South Africa. After a free Black man convinced her to move to British-controlled Cape Town, Baartman was eventually brought to London. Beginning in 1810, she was exhibited in England as the "Hottentot Venus," a freak-show attraction meant to draw in Londoners who were unfamiliar with Africans. They jeered at her large buttocks, which were exaggerated in flyers promoting the exhibition, seeing her more as a creature than as a human. In 1815, she was taken to France, where she was exhibited under similarly exploitative conditions. Baartman died that year, at the age of twenty-six. Even now, the world does not know her birth name; she lives on as Venus but not as who she really was. Yet another act of violence.

completely erased the fact that she'd taken the school system to task by exposing the vast inequality between Black and white schools. This assumption—and his willingness to share it with others—was insulting on multiple levels.

Ida wrote the minister, insisting that she meet with him in person the next time she visited Vicksburg. She arrived flanked by all five of the close friends who relayed the minister's slanderous remarks about her. It was very important that he set the record straight about her reputation. She was a single Black woman. She was a businesswoman. And she needed to make sure that her reputation was intact for both her safety and for her business. She insisted that he apologize not only to her in person but also publicly from his pulpit. She wrote the statement for him to say:

```
To Whom It May Concern:
I desire to say that any remarks I have made
reflecting on the character of Miss Ida B.
Wells are false. This I do out of deference
to her as a lady and myself as a Christian
gentleman.
```

She told him that her "good name was all that I had in the world, that I was bound to protect it from attack by those who felt that they could do so with impunity because I had no brother or father to protect it for me." She wanted him to know, "Virtue was not at all a matter of the section in which one lived; that many a slave woman had fought and died rather than yield to the pressure and temptations to which she was subjected. I had heard many tales of such." Ida emphasized, "I was one southern girl, born and bred, who had tried to keep herself spotless and morally clean as my slave mother had taught me."

Luckily for the pastor, she showed him some extra grace in writing. In her autobiography, she noted that she "will not mention his name, because he is still living and occupies an honorable position." So despite his rush to declare her unfit for polite society, the minister appears only as "Rev.—" in her recounting of the incidents.

Speaking Truth to Power

Ida's boldness often extended to explicitly political spaces, even and especially ones where Black women were often not welcome. For example, eight months after the

Illinois state senator Shelby Moore Cullom urged President William McKinley (pictured) to meet with Ida.

Woodrow Wilson agreed to meet with Ida, but their discussion produced little in the way of progress from the then president. Wilson's anti-Black ideas became more well-known to the public in the years after his 1924 death.

1913 suffrage march she defiantly integrated, Ida did another courageous thing: she went to speak to President Woodrow Wilson in person. It wasn't her first time visiting a sitting president. She had also met with President William McKinley in 1898 to talk with him about the murder of the postmaster Frazier B. Baker, a Black federal employee in Lake City, South Carolina, and the need to make lynching a federal crime. Despite hearing lip service, nothing happened.

William Monroe Trotter, who formed the National Equal Rights League (NERL) to fight against these types of injustices, was a friend of Ida's. He was also the passionate and opinionated editor of the *Boston Guardian*. Both of them were considered "militant" because they weren't willing to silently settle for second-class citizenship. Ida joined the NERL, and Trotter asked her to go with his delegation to the White House to discuss the problem with President Wilson. Ida believed Wilson's treatment of federal employees had been unequivocally wrong, too. She was disappointed in his lack of concern about whether African Americans had their rights as full citizens realized. Ida's frustration didn't come from nowhere: during his campaign, Wilson vocally supported the advancement of African Americans.

However, after he won the election, Wilson's administration reversed course: The Post Office and the Department of the Treasury were ordered to segregate. Partitions separated Black and white workers' desks. Several members of Wilson's cabinet forbade their Black secretaries and clerks from using the same restaurants and bathrooms as their white counterparts. Many Black people lost faith in their efforts to advocate for equality in their local communities while segregation was encouraged and implemented in Washington, DC.

A year passed after Ida's visit—still, the president did nothing. Ida was disappointed but not surprised. Frustrating years spent fighting for change with slow progress had inoculated her to the failings of government. Trotter was still hopeful that he could make an impact on Wilson, so he made an appointment in 1914 to visit the White House again on his own. The solo meeting was a disaster. Trotter was infuriated when President Wilson claimed that integration caused friction between colored and white clerks. The president tried to frame segregation as a benefit to Black people, because they could avoid being in humiliating situations.

Trotter's reaction to these statements got him thrown out of the White House. Once it was obvious that they would get no support from the federal government, Ida invited Trotter to speak in Chicago and stay as a guest in her home. With no friend to be found in the White House, they needed to come up with another strategy to win justice.

Throughout her life, Ida embraced direct, one-on-one advocacy. She frequently met with leaders—presidents, governors, and other officials—and spoke candidly about the injustices she saw all around her. Advocating on behalf of people who could not always walk into those rooms with her, she refused to homogenize her message or back down from her ideals.

Black Lives Matter

Today, Ida's legacy of speaking truth to power lives on in the multipronged work that Black organizers, activists, and thinkers have done. While many view Donald Trump's presidency to be a historical outlier, his tactics and rhetoric share much of those displayed by Ida's contemporary Woodrow Wilson. Wilson and Trump both openly utilized economic distress and existing racial division to tap into working-class Americans' willingness to stomach—if not outright support—destructive policies. Though the people who supported them span a range of economic backgrounds, both relied on heightened financial worries to boost their appeal.

2014 protest in Ferguson, Missouri, after the fatal shooting of Michael Brown by police officer Darren Wilson.

In 2014, when the Ferguson, Missouri, police officer Darren Wilson killed the unarmed Black teenager Michael Brown, longtime organizers and newly galvanized people alike joined to protest the deadly racism of American policing. Those early days saw a swell of public demonstrations, most of them peaceful, which were met with violent repression from the police and military. It was clear that Black people could not mourn or express frustration publicly without being in danger.

The protests grew into what is most often referred to as the Black Lives Matter movement. The specific phrase, coined by the activists Patrisse Cullors, Opal Tometi, and Alicia Garza, is also the name of a broad member-based organization with chapters around the country. A number of other groups and individuals mobilized, decrying the racism of the American criminal justice system and extrajudicial killings that often target Black people. While they were met with some open bigotry and threats of violence from police while protesting, some members of these groups were invited to the White House by President Barack Obama in February 2016.

The meeting came eighteen months after the death of Michael Brown. In the interim, efforts to reform the criminal justice system, and especially to institute some kind of accountability for officers who used fatal force against unarmed people, had swept the country. That all happened because of the young organizers who rallied around Brown, one another, and the community more broadly. Obama, who had given only tepid support for the protestors to that point, seemed to be listening: "They are much

Above: President Barack Obama hesitated to meet with leaders of the Black Lives Matter movement, only doing so eighteen months after Michael Brown's death.

better organizers than I was when I was their age, and I am confident that they are going to take America to new heights."

Civil rights leaders spanning from the late freedom rider, Martin Luther King Jr. associate, and U.S. representative John Lewis to other activists like Rev. Al Sharpton were present. But just a couple of months later, Obama again turned to what some viewed as scolding: when he spoke at a London rally filled with young activists and organizers, he warned them not to agitate too much: "Once you've highlighted an issue and brought it to people's attention . . . then you can't just keep on yelling at them," he said, noting that they shouldn't dismiss elected officials. But ultimately, Trump's election that followed a few months later bore out the organizers' predictions, not his. And their work continues.

Trump's election in 2016 saw a troubling resurgence of white supremacist sentiment reminiscent of racial backlash last seen in the late 1800s post-Reconstruction era. State governments issued new protections for Confederate monuments. Conservatives rolled out a wave of suppression efforts targeted to disenfranchise Black and brown voters. And police brutality against Black citizens continued to go unpunished by the courts. The similarities in response to Black progress have surged interest in the tactics used by Ida and her contemporaries to navigate a hostile social environment.

RECONSTRUCTION

The Reconstruction era (1865–1877) set the course for the nation's post-Civil War future, and its shortcomings defined much of Ida's life as a journalist and activist. Following the death of President Lincoln and the end of the Civil War, a sharp backlash to such progress as suffrage for freedmen emerged. Even when southern states were no longer able to legally enforce fugitive slave acts, Black people faced constant violence.

Among other horrors, the Ku Klux Klan was created during this time. Reconstruction brought with it unique threats to Black life— and a particular vitriol from white people who were unwilling to see Black people gain any semblance of rights. That kind of backlash is deeply American, so familiar now that many people have rightfully pointed to the election of Donald Trump as a direct result of racist anger about Barack Obama's presidency.

Though the protests of recent years have been unprecedented in their breadth, Black women have been speaking out against racist police violence for decades—and in ways that often angered the white people who heard them. In early 1992, the rapper Sister Souljah, born Lisa Williamson, released the album *360 Degrees of Power*. The year before, four Los Angeles police officers had severely beaten an unarmed Black man named Rodney King. Video footage of the brutality circulated, and the officers' trials the following year were a tipping point for the city. Three of the four officers were acquitted, and the jury failed to reach a verdict on one charge for the last. Almost immediately, Los Angeles experienced mass unrest, six days in which a series of protests, demonstrations, and sometimes-violent displays saw Black Angelenos express the depth of their anger at the continuing violence that the police enacted with impunity.

Within weeks of the Los Angeles uprisings, Sister Souljah appeared on a morning talk show alongside the New Jersey senator Bill Bradley and a New York congressman, Charles Rangel. In this conversation, she referred to the state of Black Americans in the country as one of constant oppression. But in a later interview, reported by the *Washington Post*, Souljah explained her empathy for the Los Angeles rioters in a way that sparked immediate backlash:

> I mean, if black people kill black people every day, why not have a week and kill white people? You understand what I'm saying? In other words, white people, this government and that mayor were well aware of the fact that black people were dying every day in Los Angeles under gang violence. So if you're a gang member and you would normally be killing somebody, why not kill a white person? Do you think that somebody thinks that white people are better, or above dying, when they would kill their own kind?

It was a shock to viewers—and to one candidate for president: William "Bill" J. Clinton. Soon after, the then presidential hopeful, who'd leaned heavily on support from Black voters, spoke to Rev. Jesse Jackson Sr.'s Rainbow Coalition. In an attempt

Sister Souljah. The American artist, author, and musician received criticism for comments she made supporting the at times violent protests in response to the 1991 beating of Rodney King by Los Angeles police. Her remarks were condemned by then candidate Bill Clinton, in what many saw as a political move to distance himself from the Black American community.

to balance his Black support with white voters' perception that he was too close to the "radical" Rev. Jackson, Clinton took the opportunity to repudiate Sister Souljah—also in attendance as a guest of the conference.

Clinton made a pithy, ahistorical comparison: "If you took the words 'white' and 'black,' and you reversed them, you might think [the Ku Klux Klan grand wizard] David Duke was giving that speech." He was also unreceptive to Rev. Jackson's assertion that Souljah had been trying to express the extreme repression that Black people in America had faced since the country's inception. To this day, the term "Sister Souljah moment" carries a specific meaning in political parlance: when a politician has one such moment, it refers to them distancing themselves from a member of their party or group whom others might see as an extremist.

Whether or not her confrontation with reporters was ultimately successful, Sister Souljah forced a national conversation about the resentment that injustice can breed. In that context, it's hardly surprising that her name is invoked when describing the callous moves some politicians make.

Sister Souljah, like many others, was following in the long tradition set by Black women like Ida B. Wells to stand tall and let their voices be heard by those in power, even in the face of severe criticism and potential loss of work or money.

Working and Protesting Alone

Often, Ida took on the challenge and sacrifice of her work without anyone else's assistance. In 1930, Ida B. Wells was almost sixty-eight years old and had been working for over fifty years. By then, she could have felt that it was time to slow down. But she was disgusted with the male political leadership and decided to jump into the Illinois state senate race as an independent candidate. Without support from a major political organization, Ida and Ferdinand funded most of her campaign themselves. They printed posters, newsletters, and letters, and distributed them all over the district.

Despite the grueling schedule of giving at least two speeches a day, Ida lost the race by a wide margin. However, her run for state senate was historymaking, as Ida was one of the first Black women in the nation to run for public office. Getting in the race was a victory in and of itself. She was a Black woman who had challenged a racist and patriarchal society to reject its assumption that Black Americans would be held subordinate indefinitely.

By the time Ida B. Wells reached her mid-sixties, she had been a firsthand witness to the realities of slavery, the freedom and hope of Reconstruction, the terror of post-Reconstruction, the implementation of Jim Crow laws, the Spanish-American War, World War I, segregation, mass migration, riots, and women fighting and winning the right to vote.

Ida's determination and insistence on positive action over reconciliation was not always welcome within the civil rights organizations of her time. She did not possess the temperament for glad-handing and standing aside while her people "waited their turn." But despite feeling alone and misunderstood at times during her personal fight for justice, she was firmly entrenched in the great social and cultural change seen during her lifetime and beyond. Of the organizations she played a personal role in founding, two are still functional to this day: the National Association of Colored Women's Clubs (NACWC) and the National Association for the Advancement of Colored People (NAACP).

Modern Mavericks

BREE NEWSOME

In 2015, months into the swell of activism that followed the death of Michael Brown, and weeks after the white supremacist Dylann Roof murdered nine Black people at a Bible study in Mother Emanuel AME Church in Charleston, a South Carolina artist named Brittany "Bree" Newsome (now Bree Newsome Bass) did something that still stands as a powerful image even years later. The day before, President Obama had given a speech calling for the Confederate flag to be removed from the South Carolina statehouse. Newsome had decided even before Obama's speech that she would scale the flagpole to remove the flag herself. And she did.

She raised it triumphantly, dominating over a potent symbol of centuries of white supremacy. The visual of the young Black woman scaling a thirty-foot pole to remove the flag was as controversial as it was powerful. Newsome was met with waves of harassment, as well as condemnation from the governor, Nikki Haley. (Haley would later go on to sign a bill removing the flag.) Even so, Newsome didn't regret her decision. Two years later, she told *Vox*, "I grew up with my grandmother who was raised in Greenville, who told me about her experiences seeing the Ku Klux Klan beat her neighbor and things like that. The massacre in Charleston brought a refocus on the flag." History is never too far removed.

A Charlotte, North Carolina-based filmmaker and activist, Bree Newsome reached acclaim when she climbed the flagpole at the South Carolina state capitol building to protest the state's display of the Confederate States of America's battleflag. Newsome scaled the flagpole near the capitol and removed the flag from its perch. She and an aide were immediately arrested.

COLIN KAEPERNICK
MUHAMMAD ALI
TOMMIE SMITH AND JOHN CARLOS

The name Colin Kaepernick now conjures an era that might feel like it was eons ago. The National Football League (NFL) has moved past him; the rapper Jay-Z teamed up with the league in 2019 to help bolster social justice and entertainment initiatives. It would seem that everything was neatly tied up.

But even if that were all true, it wasn't the case at first. Before the NFL found indirect ways to talk about injustice that fit within the comfort zones of the owners and many fans, a significant chunk of the sports world turned on the San Francisco 49ers quarterback.

Kaepernick silently protested the injustice of police brutality—and racism in America more broadly—during the playing of the national anthem before each game. As his protest started to attract attention, Kaepernick became the target of nationwide ire from other players in the mostly Black league, as well as from the media and NFL fans. Some conservatives claimed he was disrespecting veterans with his protest; others said he had no right to protest because of his salary and position as a professional athlete, and should only be allowed to entertain, not cause a ruckus.

In 2019, Rihanna declined an invitation to perform at the Super Bowl, citing her support for Kaepernick as the reason.

In many of these complaints, even the ones that did not seem obviously racist, there was often contempt toward Kaepernick for the simple fact of his being a young Black man pointing out an inconvenient truth. Even other Black athletes were torn. He didn't immediately receive wide support, and his method of silently kneeling while on the sidelines of the football field was considered too radical by some.

But the years after his original 2016 season protest saw a rise in athletes' activism across different sports and leagues. Among other 2020 initiatives to acknowledge racial inequality, the NFL printed "End Racism" in the end zones. However, Kaepernick himself, despite reaching rare heights on the field prior to his demonstrations, has not secured another contract in the NFL as of the end of 2020. But the impact of his early actions—and his continued commitment to the causes he believes in—ripples out beyond Kaepernick, the NFL, and the country.

Kaepernick was denied the opportunity to play in the NFL during the peak of his career in much the same way that Muhammad Ali was arrested, found guilty of draft evasion, and stripped of his boxing titles in 1966 at twenty-four years old. He was unable to box for four of his prime athletic years while banned from the sport for his refusal to fight in the Vietnam War. Ali went on to become known as "the Greatest" based on the later years of his athletic career, a time when most in his field would be considered over-the-hill.

Two years later, the gold medalist Tommie Smith and the bronze medalist John Carlos each raised a black-gloved fist during the playing of the national anthem at their medal ceremony at the 1968 Olympics. The gesture, taken by many as a reference to the Black Power

movement, is still seen as one of the most overtly political demonstrations in Olympic history. The 200-meter track stars Smith and Carlos were fed up. Fed up with Ali's exile, fed up with the lack of access to good housing in their urban communities, fed up with the casual racism of the sports world. And they were punished greatly for it. A familiar pattern played out: Smith and Carlos were seen as good enough to *compete* for the United States, but they were not deserving of the right to point out the oppression that they, and other Black people, experienced in their country.

They were expelled from the Games and mostly ostracized from the sports world. They were met with racist criticism on sports networks, in newspapers, and in magazines. Their families received death threats. Over five decades later, their images have been somewhat rehabilitated by the passage of time and growing support for their positions, but the toll of those lost years cannot be undone.

All these athletes transcended their sport and became more well-known as a

result of their courage to speak out against injustice. They share this with Ida, who criticized the Memphis school system and then lost her job. When she spoke out against lynching, she lost her printing press and her life as she knew it. As a result of death threats, she never lived in the South again.

Speaking out about injustice can be a lonely experience and often comes with the loss of things that one holds dear. But the question must be asked: Is it better to be silent and endure hardship, or is it better to speak out and possibly effect change? Standing out and speaking out alone is something few are willing to do. And the ones who do often become historymakers, as Ida has. The attention she has gained posthumously surpasses the level of appreciation that she experienced while alive. During her life she was considered so controversial and "militant" that many times she stood alone.

Organizing Together

Many people who face a hostile social environment form or join groups and organizations in order to collectively combat injustice rather than try to do things alone. Ida was no different. Even though she fought against the railroad on her own in the early 1880s, she was part of a community that was supportive. In Memphis, she belonged to social groups called lyceums, where people gathered to share creative works and political ideas with like-minded individuals. The environment energized Ida, providing an outlet she did not find within the confines of her teaching career. It was where she began to realize the power of collective action and see her own potential as a leader.

After she left Memphis, she both founded and participated in a variety of organizations, including but not limited to the National Association of Colored Women, the National Association for the Advancement of Colored People, the Ida B. Wells Club, Universal Negro Improvement Association, the National Equal Rights League, the Negro Fellowship League, the Alpha Suffrage Club, and the Illinois Equal Suffrage Association. Engaging in and exchanging ideas, talents, perspectives, and tactics, Ida was part of a critical moment in the United States' progression to a more perfect union.

Ida B. moved to New York City in 1892 and started working with T. Thomas Fortune on his *New York Age* newspaper. Thomas also introduced her to the nascent National Afro-American Council, of which Ida became the inaugural secretary. The group was formed in 1898 after a spate of violent lynchings and is considered the nation's first

T. Thomas Fortune, depicted in *The Afro-American Press and Its Editors*, circa 1891. Fortune was the leading Black economist of his time and the publisher of the *New York Age*, America's leading Black newspaper of its time.

T. THOMAS FORTUNE.

nationwide civil rights organization. They lobbied actively for the passage of a federal antilynching law (there have been over two hundred attempts within the last century to pass such laws—the most recent introduced by the 116th Congress in 2019).

Ida's travels in this period had a profound impact on her worldview and understanding of what was possible. An 1893 trip to the United Kingdom opened her eyes to a more progressive society, strengthened by women coming together to form social clubs that elevated their voices and provided real influence over politics. When she arrived in Chicago for the World's Fair later that year, a women's club was formed in Chicago and Ida was selected as chairman. In September it was chartered as the Ida B. Wells Club. In 1896, Ida cofounded the National Association of Colored Women, and Mary Church Terrell was elected as the first president.

More than a decade later, in 1909, Ida became one of the founders of the National Association for the Advancement of Colored People (NAACP), along with W. E. B. Du Bois and Mary Church Terrell. The group was formed in response to a Springfield, Illinois, race riot.

But Ida quickly grew frustrated with the organization when she realized that most of its leaders were wealthy white moderates who wanted to "study" the race problem rather than get involved in concrete action and activism. She considered their approach to be too passive and gradually disengaged from their supposed mission. She also was insulted when the organization adopted her antilynching platform

LIFTING AS WE CLIMB

Founded under the motto "Lifting as We Climb," the National Association of Colored Women (later renamed the National Association of Colored Women's Clubs) advocated for women's rights as well as sought to "uplift" and improve the status of all African Americans. During the early years of the organization, the largely educated and middle-class constituency supported temperance, positive images of women through moral purity, and women's suffrage—issues also pursued by white women's groups. But they eventually expanded to include many social services targeted to the needs of economically disadvantaged communities, including raising money for kindergartens, libraries, orphanages, and homes for the elderly. The organization also raised awareness around lynching, segregation, and other issues specific to the Black community.

Banner with the motto of the National Association of Colored Women's Clubs.

without giving her the credit she deserved and then selected the younger W. E. B. Du Bois over her to edit its national *Crisis* magazine. The selection was made despite Ida's status as one of the most prolific and well-known journalists of her time.

Despite Ida's differences with this early iteration of the NAACP, its work in the years that followed is not to be ignored. Rosa Parks, Medgar Evers, Thurgood Marshall, and thousands of other activists have been part of the NAACP in the fight for equal rights in voting, housing, education, health care, and public accommodations.

After gradually disengaging from the NAACP over a few years, Ida got involved in the National Equal Rights League (NERL) in 1913 and worked with William Monroe Trotter, the editor of the *Boston Guardian*. The organization pursued equal rights through the courts, arguing that these institutions were more sympathetic to Black rights than federal or state governments. During World War I, the NERL took up Ida's signature cause to make lynching a federal crime. It was this effort that brought her and Trotter to President Woodrow Wilson's White House with a 25,000-signature petition in hand. Wilson was unmoved, and more than a century later Congress has still failed to pass law on this measure.

The concept of unionizing in order to participate in collective bargaining has also been something that Black people have engaged in for over a century. In fact, Ida B. Wells wrote an entire pamphlet titled *The Arkansas Race Riot* about a group of sharecroppers in Elaine, Arkansas, who tried to form a union in 1919. Their demand for fair compensation for their crop and attempt to organize around it was met with violence—dozens of deaths and extensive destruction of property.

The spirit of rising up against economic injustice still rings true today, from the 2019 teachers' strikes that took place in several states to sick-outs at Amazon warehouses taking place in 2020. Collective action has a long history.

During the late 1950s to mid-1960s, several organizations were formed in order to fight against racial oppression. These include the Student Nonviolent Coordinating Committee (SNCC), the Black Panthers, and the Southern Christian Leadership Conference (SCLC), just to name a few.

In 1971, another organization formed that still is functioning today. Operation PUSH (People United to Serve Humanity) began with the focus of uniting people in the fight for economic equality for African Americans. Operation PUSH, which was established by Rev. Jesse Jackson Sr., expanded into areas of social and political development. Based in Ida's adopted home of Chicago, the organization merged with the Rainbow Coalition to create the Rainbow/PUSH Coalition, and has been working on campaigns ranging from antipoverty advocacy to voter registration and enfranchisement for more than forty years.

When the Reverend Martin Luther King Jr. was assassinated in 1968, trusted associate Jesse Jackson Sr. was at his side. Jackson went on to become a civil rights icon in his own right, founding the Rainbow/ PUSH social justice organization and becoming a serious contender for the Democratic Party's nomination in the 1988 presidential election.

A Chicago-based politician and civil rights leader, Oscar De Priest was the first African American elected to the United States Congress in the twentieth century.

In 1913, Illinois granted women limited suffrage. Ida saw a rare opportunity to fully utilize the force of both of her life's great causes: combating racism and sexism. She founded the Alpha Suffrage Club in Chicago, and it quickly developed a block system to canvass the neighborhood and register African American women to vote. Their work saw immediate returns in 1914 as Oscar De Priest was elected as the city's first Black alderman. In 1928, he became the first African American congressman elected to the House of Representatives from a northern state and a national symbol for racial pride.

After fighting for so many years to gain respect and equal rights as citizens of the United States, an African American movement focused on the African diaspora took hold during the second decade of the twentieth century. Marcus Garvey formed the Universal Negro Improvement Association in 1914. Its motto, "One God! One Aim! One Destiny!," and its slogan, "Africa for the Africans, at home and abroad!," reflected its global orientation.

Ida got involved because she truly believed that Black people needed to be self-sufficient. On top of that, Marcus Garvey was not intimidated by her

The controversial Jamaican-born activist, publisher, journalist, and philosopher Marcus Garvey became known for his view that Black Americans could not truly be free until they had achieved full self-sufficiency. Many interpreted this as a separatist ideology. He was also an advocate of Pan-Africanism, the idea that all people of African descent should unite to build power and create distinct spaces of their own for safety and prosperity.

outspokenness. He invited Ida to his meeting in December 1918, and she was selected as a delegate to attend the group's 1919 Paris Peace Conference in France as a follow-up to the end of World War I. Unfortunately, she and close ally Madam C. J. Walker, who had financially supported antilynching work, were both denied passports to attend.

Black activism stretches across the globe. In 1977, Randall Robinson founded TransAfrica Forum, which focused on influencing American foreign policy toward Africa and the Caribbean. Going in the opposite direction, in 2019, Ghana implemented the Year of Return, in remembrance of the four hundred years since Africans were first enslaved in what would become the British colonies that later formed the United States. The country welcomed African Americans back "home," and many took advantage of that offer in response to their feeling that gaining full equality in the United States was more of a distant dream than a potential reality.

Taking Control of Our Narrative

When Ida wrote about the realities of her friends being lynched, she was countering false narratives about Black people. She took control of the narrative and presented the Black perspective to counter propaganda that framed Black people as biologically or sociologically inferior, dangerous, and violent.

The prevailing narrative at the time was that Black men were sexual predators who targeted white women and therefore deserved to die in a most brutal way. Other victims of lynching had been framed as dangers to the social order, specifically threatening to white people, or robbers. Horrific acts against Black people were normalized over time: torture, collecting their teeth and bones as souvenirs, or even burning them alive for the enjoyment of spectators.

Ida investigated these atrocities with the goal of humanizing their victims. Time and time again, she found that the victims were misidentified scapegoats targeted to be punished for a crime that was committed by someone else or swept up in an act of terror intended to institute social control over unwanted Black communities and neighbors. When Ida wrote her articles in the *Free Speech* about the lynching of the three grocers, she highlighted how the murders' implication of violence against any Black person, at any time, kept the surrounding community terrorized and economically disenfranchised for a generation.

Her landmark pamphlets *Southern Horrors* in 1892 and *A Red Record* in 1895 outlined in great detail individual cases and statistics to convey the vast scale of America's lynching problem. Pioneering what is now called "data journalism," Ida collected this information from a wide variety of sources. She scoured articles by white correspondents and in white-owned newspapers, combining those findings with the statistics she was able to pull from sources that she ultimately democratized by putting them in one place. In *A Red Record*, she listed the various "crimes" committed that resulted in lynching:

```
Rape, attempted rape, alleged rape, suspicion
of rape, murder, alleged murder, alleged
complicity in murder, murderous assault,
attempted murder, attempted robbery, arson,
incendiarism, alleged stock poisoning,
poisoning wells, alleged poisoning wells,
burglary, wife beating, self-defense,
suspected robbery, assault and battery,
insulting whites, malpractice, alleged barn
burning, stealing, unknown offense, no
offense, race prejudice
```

And in 1899's *Lynch Law in Georgia*, she wrote thus to summarize the murders of over a dozen people:

```
The real purpose of these savage
demonstrations is to teach the Negro that in
the South he has no rights that the law will
enforce. Samuel Hose was burned to teach the
Negroes that no matter what a white man does
to them, they must not resist.
```

A year later, in 1900, she wrote *Mob Rule in New Orleans*, which chronicled the widespread mob violence inflicted on the Black community and the horrible demise of Robert Charles, who was murdered in retaliation for defending himself against a police officer.

Ida B. Wells's *Lynch Law in Georgia,* a document used to inform political and organization leaders about the scope of unchecked violence against Black Americans in the late nineteenth century.

Lynch Law
in Georgia.

BY

IDA B. WELLS=BARNETT

A Six-Weeks' Record in the Center of Southern Civilization,
As Faithfully Chronicled by the "Atlanta Journal"
and the "Atlanta Constitution."

ALSO THE FULL REPORT OF LOUIS P. LE VIN,

The Chicago Detective Sent to Investigate the Burning of
Samuel Hose, the Torture and Hanging of Elijah Strick-
land, the Colored Preacher, and the Lynching
of Nine Men for Alleged Arson.

This Pamphlet is Circulated by Chicago Colored Citizens.

2939 Princeton Avenue, Chicago.

THE GREAT MIGRATION

The Great Migration saw six million African Americans leaving the South beginning in the early twentieth century. Many fled the region to escape the kinds of racial violence that Ida spent her life fighting. These journeys echoed the exodus from Memphis that was made following her editorial about the city's lynchings. The Great Migration resulted in a wider dispersal of Black people across the country, in places ranging from the Northeast to the West Coast, all in search of something approximating safety.

In 1917, she wrote *The East St. Louis Massacre: The Greatest Outrage of the Century*, a chronicle of the horrific violence against an entire Black community. She also outlined oft-overlooked tensions that existed in the American North, where the first waves of the Great Migration tested the Union states' full belief in their cause.

During World War I, with the shortage of workers in the North, there was an effort to employ recent migrants from the South. This led to labor displacement in certain areas and a fight for equal wages. In East St. Louis, Illinois, this battle between the white community and Black migrants led to the death and destruction of an entire Black community. The National Guard was called into the area, but they proceeded to do nothing to protect the Black residents. Thousands of people were killed, and those that survived were displaced and lost all of their property.

Ida went around in the aftermath of the riot and interviewed people firsthand to learn what had happened to them. She then wrote her pamphlet describing the reality of the situation and met with Illinois governor Frank Lowden in order to make sure that those who created the situation would be held accountable.

By investigating the situation herself and chronicling personal accounts of what happened, Ida was taking control of the narrative. Instead of allowing white people to spin and skew reality to justify their annihilation of Black people, she documented the brutal truth about the violence being inflicted on the Black community. Her influence helped reduce retaliatory sentencing for a few Black people but did little to have white instigators punished for the destruction.

Ida's project of amassing the details of anti-Black crime nationwide through data journalism continued when she went down to Arkansas in 1920 to investigate the deaths of a slew of Black sharecroppers and the sentencing of twelve to death row. By talking to people herself, she learned that their supposed crime had been an effort to form a labor union and secure better pay for cotton industry workers. One of their meetings had been besieged, and a white person died in the fighting that ensued. The sharecroppers present at the meeting were accused of murder, and hundreds of innocent Black people were murdered in retaliation. Their property was destroyed, and descendants of the victims insist to this day that a great land theft took place.

Ida's pamphlet *The Arkansas Race Riot* countered the prevailing narrative at the time—that the whites raiding Black people's property were simply defending themselves. She told the story from the Black people's point of view, leaving behind a firsthand account that still survives to this day. Elaine is still struggling to reconcile

JOHN H. JOHNSON

In 1942, John H. Johnson was an office clerk at a Chicago life insurance company. He used a $500 loan to start the Johnson Publishing Company, printing the *Negro Digest* later that year and eventually adding the famed *Ebony* and *Jet* magazines. But Johnson Publishing also brought *The Ebony Cookbook*, by the columnist Freda DeKnight, and *The New Ebony Cookbook*, by the author Charlotte Lyons, into homes around the country. Through standard news, commentary, or preserving Black food traditions, Johnson Publishing helped chronicle Black life in America.

with that past. An uptick in interest has seen these riots come under renewed scrutiny in recent years, but the history was largely buried for nearly a century. And almost nothing has been done yet to bring about justice for the victims or their families who had their lives and wealth stolen.

Many people have followed Ida's example of taking control of disputed history—most often shaped by the wealthy and powerful—and telling those stories through the lens of Black people's perspective. From the first Black newspaper, *Freedom's Journal*, started in 1827, to Frederick Douglass establishing the *North Star* newspaper in 1847, to John H. Johnson founding the Johnson Publishing Company in 1942 (the publisher of *Ebony* and *Jet* magazines), Black people have had to write, create, and own dozens of other media outlets to have their own stories heard.

In more recent history, several Black women have emerged as leaders in creating corrective works. Nikole Hannah-Jones of the *New York Times Magazine* spearheaded the narrative-altering "1619 Project," which reexamined the legacy of slavery in the United States and its ongoing impact on the structures of the country. She won a Pulitzer Prize for Commentary in 2020, the same year that Ida was awarded her posthumous Special Citation.

In 2016, Ava DuVernay produced the Netflix documentary *13th*, which explored the history of racial inequality in the United States, focusing on the legislative decisions that have resulted in the nation's disproportionately Black prison population. Three years later, DuVernay created the series *When They See Us*, which told the story of the "Central Park Five" from their perspective and reframed them as the "Exonerated Five."

Pop culture, cinema, and storytelling have a huge role to play in opening new eyes to the individual stories that make up America's despicable history of race-based oppression, but the work cannot stop there. Cultural institutions are emerging nationwide to bring the African American experience to traditional platforms that have been slow to adapt. Under the leadership of Lonnie G. Bunch III, the Smithsonian Institution created the National Museum of African American History and Culture in Washington, DC. It opened in 2016 and showcases the African American story's impact on American and world history, including an exhibit on Ida.

In 2018, the Equal Justice Initiative opened the Legacy Museum: From Slavery to Mass Incarceration and the National Memorial for Peace and Justice in Montgomery, Alabama. It humanizes the stories of slavery, mass incarceration, and lynching that

EXONERATED
~~CENTRAL PARK~~ FIVE

The infamous Central Park Five case divided New York City—and the whole country—in 1989. Following the assault and brutal rape of a white woman who had been jogging through the Manhattan park, five Black and Latino teenagers were rounded up by the NYPD and coerced into confessing to the crime after at least seven hours of interrogation each. The national press played into stereotypes about Black criminality in its coverage of the case, swaying public opinion against the boys. Most notably, a local real estate guru named Donald Trump took out a full-page newspaper ad calling for the deaths of the so-called "wolf pack."

Despite the evidence against them being circumstantial and often contradictory, four of the boys—Antron McCray, Yusef Salaam, Kevin Richardson, and Raymond Santana—all ultimately served between six and seven years in juvenile facilities. Korey Wise, known then as Kharey, served thirteen years and eight months in various state prisons. In 2001, at the Auburn Correctional Facility in New York, he met a man named Matias Reyes. Convicted of serial rape and murder, Reyes later confessed to the 1989 assault of Tricia Meili, the Central Park jogger. The original five, who had always maintained that they were innocent, would have their convictions vacated in 2002. They sued the city the following year and received a settlement over ten years later, in 2014.

THOMAS MOSS~CALVIN McDOWELL~
WILLIAM HENRY STEWART
THE LYNCHING AT THE CURVE

In March of 1892, business partners Thomas Moss, Calvin McDowell and William Henry Stewart, were arrested for defending themselves against an attack on their store, *The People's Grocery*. The white competitor and the deputy sheriffs he hired were met with gunfire. Several deputies were wounded but survived. Nevertheless, Moss, McDowell, and Stewart, were taken from the downtown jail by masked vigilantes, dragged to a deserted railroad yard in north Memphis and shot to death.

Memphis was thrown into a state of shock. Moss, McDowell and Stewart were part of a thriving black community at *The Curve*, where most attended the same church and belonged to the same lodges. Twenty-one-year-old Calvin McDowell was a member of the Tennessee Rifles, a black military organization respected for its service protecting the city during the virulent Yellow Fever epidemics of the 1870s.

Thomas Moss was one of the first black postal carriers in Memphis. Activist Mary Church Terrell, deeply affected by his murder, described "Tom Moss" as one of her best childhood friends. Thomas and his wife Betty were Ida B. Wells' closest friends. She was godmother to their three-year-old daughter Maurine. Betty was at the time, expecting the family's second child.

(Continued on other side)

stain American history while avoiding the stereotypes and false information that often infect the discussion. The Equal Justice Initiative and other local organizations, such as the Lynching Sites Project of Memphis, place markers throughout the country to honor the victims of lynchings alongside their personal stories—applying faces, names, and details to historical instances of people's deaths at the hands of racist mobs.

As for the three owners of the People's Grocery who were killed outside Memphis, the Mount Zion Cemetery restoration project in Memphis honored their memories with a marker in 2019.

National Memorial for Peace and Justice.

Above, right: Historical marker for Thomas Moss, Calvin McDowell, and William Henry Stewart.

We Shall Not Be Moved

Despite years of progress in the wake of Ida's work, America continues to tolerate efforts to silence and disrespect Black women. But in the face of that harsh reality, there are still brilliant examples of contemporary figures carrying on Ida B. Wells's example of resilience in the face of all obstacles.

Ida B. Wells was a powerful political figure in her time, but she never personally served in an elected political office. Despite that, her influence outside government as a journalist and organizer was immense. With both efforts for racial equity and women's suffrage taking place within her own lifetime, Ida was perhaps fated to fight for the advancement of, rather than personally benefit from, the great causes of her time. Today Black women, along with others, are empowered to make change directly from within the halls of power.

It is to everyone's benefit that racially targeted lynching—while by no means eradicated—is far less prevalent today than it was in Ida's time. But a newer scourge, that of disproportionately Black gun victimization, has sprung up in its place. The United States in particular has seen gun violence spiral into an epidemic over the first

MAXINE WATERS

California congresswoman Maxine Waters is one of those heroines who carry the torch for equal rights and representation in the twenty-first century. A frequent target for President Donald Trump's stoking of racial and gender resentments, she stood strong in defense of herself and her constituents. She constantly spoke out against his policies, pointed out his personal flaws, and refused to be silent, despite facing incredible levels of criticism and even threats. Waters faced vilification and death threats as she stepped forward as a leader in the effort to impeach Donald Trump for ethical lapses and incompetence. Her cause ultimately succeeded on January 16, 2020, when Trump became the third United States president in history to be impeached.

While a flight attendant and part-time activist based in Atlanta, Georgia, Lucy McBath lost her son to gun violence in a 2012 shooting. Her subsequent campaign for stronger gun laws, fueled by personal tragedy, built into a successful run for the United States House of Representatives in 2018.

few decades of the twenty-first century. In 2016, gun violence was the second leading individual cause of death for children and adolescents in America. And that spate of violence hits Black and brown children at an even more alarming rate: between 2013 and 2019, Black and Hispanic teens made up fifteen percent of the K–12 school population but were twenty-five percent of gun violence victims on school grounds. In Ida's adopted Chicago home, a study found Hispanic children and Black children faced much greater odds (seventy-four percent and 112 percent higher, respectively) of being exposed to gun violence than their white neighbors.

That tremendous burden has also led to remarkable bravery from women of color as they've stepped up to fix the problems that plague the country. Lucy McBath was born in Joliet, Illinois, just outside of Ida's adopted city of Chicago. McBath is also the daughter of Lucien Holman—himself a former president of an Illinois chapter of the NAACP. She studied political science in college and interned for future governor Douglas Wilder in Virginia, but she ultimately worked as a flight attendant at Delta Air Lines as she raised her family in Atlanta, Georgia. In 2012, McBath's seventeen-year-old son, Jordan Davis, was murdered at a gas station in Jacksonville, Florida. Michael Dunn, a forty-five-year-old white man, had been enraged by the "thug music" Davis and his friends were playing in their car. Dunn shot his handgun into the car, hitting Davis in his legs, aorta, and lungs, and continued shooting even as the car pulled away.

Six years after the death of her son, McBath ran for Congress in Georgia's sixth congressional district. With a platform that included gun law reform, McBath won the congressional seat.

SYBRINA FULTON

Like McBath, Sybrina Fulton was prompted to turn her grief into action after losing a son to racist violence. The mother of slain Florida teenager Trayvon Martin, whose death at the hands of George Zimmerman catalyzed an activist movement around the country, Fulton announced a bid for county commissioner in Miami-Dade County in 2019. In 2020, with the support of other mothers including McBath, Fulton officially qualified to run, and later ended up losing the race by less than one percent.

2020 Black Lives Matter protest in New York, NY.

In 2018, a longtime attorney named Stacey Abrams ran for governor of Georgia against Brian Kemp, then secretary of state, which meant he was in charge of elections and voter registration. Kemp refused all pressure to recuse himself from his position for the election and was allowed to run despite the conflict of interest inherent in administering his own election. He implemented numerous barriers targeted at denying the vote to groups projected to turn out strongly for Abrams (especially African American voters). Kemp "won" the election by fifty thousand votes.

Abrams refused to officially concede the race, and shortly thereafter announced the creation of Fair Fight Action, a nonprofit organization that combats voter suppression techniques. She sued the secretary of state and state election board in federal court, a lawsuit that was ongoing as of October 2020. In the interim, Abrams maintained a high profile in national politics and was even considered as a potential vice presidential candidate for Democratic presidential nominee Joe Biden.

Even now, it often seems Black women frequently find ourselves fighting alone in the push for recognition. The Black Lives Matter movement, founded in 2013, grew out of mounting frustration with police violence against the Black community. Started by three Black women, Black Lives Matter ushered in a wave of national activism. The organization, with the simple affirmation at its core, was initially met with skepticism by those who believed accusations of racism across the country were overstated.

The group's founding was yet another example of Black women's refusal to be silenced, sidelined, or ignored when it comes to having equal rights under the law. In the years that followed, the election of Donald Trump would once again prove the nation's deep and abiding devaluing of Black lives. As protests reignited following the May 25, 2020, police killing of George Floyd in Minnesota, Black women organizing with Black Lives Matter, Black Youth Project 100, Movement for Black Lives, and countless other organizations continue to fight for the dignity and safety of *all* Black people.

Beginning with the suffrage movement, white women have repeatedly fought for "women's rights" in a way that prioritizes their needs over those of all women. Many white women did not want Black people to get the right to vote, even as Black women were willing to work alongside them. During the 1970s movement for women's liberation, white women advocated for concerns that didn't affect Black women nearly as much. For example, Black women had been working—whether under the involuntary conditions of slavery or as sharecroppers and later domestics—since our arrival in this country. White women's fight to integrate themselves into the workplaces that their husbands and brothers and fathers occupied simply didn't resonate. Black women worked in their *homes*.

While moments of tension arise around the divide between Black and white women's and civil rights movements, some efforts have been made by various organizations to bridge the gap a bit. In 2020, the Rose Parade featured a suffrage float in celebration of the centennial of the passage of the Nineteenth Amendment. I was asked to ride on the float in honor of my great-grandmother, alongside the descendants of other suffrage leaders Elizabeth Cady Stanton, Frederick Douglass, Susan B. Anthony, and Harriet Tubman.

The fact that those of us who are three to five generations removed from the early leaders of the suffrage movement can meet, interact, and work with each other shows the level of improvement that this country has experienced. Yet there is still a long way to go before any of us can claim there to be true equality across the board. Having a few exceptional Black people overcome the unique obstacles that we face as a community is a sign not of absolute equality but of heroic feats by select individuals.

Self-Determination, the Law, and Politics

Black people have often taken to "making a way out of no way." We built our own postsecondary schools, now known as Historically Black Colleges and Universities (HBCUs). We started our own civic and social organizations, businesses, and business networks. We created our own guidebooks to promote and support our own institutions and ourselves. These were all part of myriad survival techniques that have been employed to maintain Black dignity and independence.

At the start of the twentieth century, Ida and her attorney husband, Ferdinand, both sought to look outside the community to help change the laws that kept Black people unequal. In order to have this they needed to not only have the right to vote but also to get involved in politics. Some of Ida's inspiration to advocate with the law might have come from the example her father set during Reconstruction. When the Fifteenth Amendment was passed in 1870, Black men were given the right to vote. Her father and many men around him earnestly engaged in political talk and exercised their newly found right.

HOLDING POLICE ACCOUNTABLE

In 1909 a penniless Black man named Will James, who was known as "Frog," was arrested after the body of a white woman was found in an alley in Cairo, Illinois. Frank Davis, the sheriff of Alexander County, was involved in the hanging of James. He allowed a mob to take the prisoner to his certain death. With no due process of law, James was hanged from an electric pole and hundreds of bullets were pumped into him before his head was cut off.

If Ida B. Wells and other Black leaders had not put pressure on Governor Charles S. Deneen, the sheriff probably would have gotten away with this negligence. However, Ida traveled to Cairo and spent two days there talking to Black people in town to gather facts about what had actually occurred. Many were scared to say anything against Sheriff Davis because they had to live among those who had committed or sanctioned the murder of Frog. In Springfield, Ida testified in front of Governor Deneen and argued that the sheriff had violated his duty and knowingly released a prisoner into an assured death.

A sheriff of a town was legally obligated to protect its inmates from a mob, and Davis had not done that. If he got away with releasing someone to an assured death, then Ida felt there was no point in even pretending to have a law enforcement department. A few days after the hearing, Governor Deneen issued his verdict to not reinstate the sheriff. The impact of this decision was far-reaching. It was the first time that someone in Illinois who was complicit in a lynching was actually punished. This changed the way accused prisoners were handled in Illinois. When a sheriff saw signs of trouble with a mob, he would immediately call the governor for troops.

Governor Charles S. Deneen.

Though she didn't yet have that right herself, Ida made her voice heard in a different way: in 1909, she testified in front of Illinois governor Charles S. Deneen to urge the permanent removal of a corrupt sheriff, Frank Davis of Cairo, Illinois, who had aided in the murder of an innocent Black man.

Many individuals and organizations have worked to hold law enforcement accountable since Ida's years. The NAACP's Legal Defense and Educational Fund was set up to fight against institutional racism. The Southern Poverty Law Center, the Equal Justice Initiative, the Sentencing Project, and many other organizations focus on assisting and defending the most disenfranchised in our society.

In the tradition of his grandparents, my father, Donald L. Duster, ran a social service agency in Chicago for over two decades. One program that was instituted was First Defense Legal Aid, which was a network of attorneys who volunteered to provide legal counsel to young people who had been arrested. The attorneys went to police stations and worked on behalf of the mostly young Black and brown males who had been arrested and did not know how to defend themselves.

Housing and Support

Throughout her life, Ida constantly straddled two worlds. She interacted with and worked with some of the most well-known leaders of the time, but she also had no problem working one-on-one with some of the most downtrodden or disenfranchised of her community. Ida often visited young prison inmates, who told her how their inability to find work had led to their troubles. Chicago didn't offer the men as much opportunity as they hoped. It seemed to Ida that Black men were only welcomed by saloons, pool rooms, and gambling houses, confining them to environments that by their nature attracted undue attention from law enforcement. They were essentially entrapped right from the start. Ida felt in her heart that whatever outsized criminal element existed within Chicago's Black neighborhoods was exacerbated by the failure to provide alternative activities to attract young men's attention.

She and Ferdinand opened the Negro Fellowship League in 1910 at 2830 South State Street, where it operated for almost three years, before it moved to the location where it would remain until its close in 1920. My great-grandfather Ferdinand was assistant state's attorney for Cook County during the first two years the League was

open. Many of his clients were exactly the kinds of otherwise promising young Black men who needed just one step up to improve their long-term prospects. They needed a temporary place to sleep, a library to help hone their work skills, and employment services to aid their search for honest work.

Institutions designed to help the most vulnerable people in society were nothing new, but building one that granted access to young Black people was far from the norm. Family, friends, and informal associations have held disenfranchised populations up through the ages, but the terrible history of the African American experience places many of us at a remarkable disadvantage. Generations of enslavement, disenfranchisement, destruction and theft of our property, and government policies that created barriers to the accumulation of Black wealth are challenges not equally shared across racial lines.

My great-grandparents Ida and Ferdinand were determined to work on behalf of those who defended themselves in the face of terror. Through their Negro Fellowship League, they helped individuals such as Steve Green, a young man from Arkansas who had previously worked on a plantation. He and the owner got into a fight that ended when Green accidentally killed the man in self-defense. Knowing that he would be lynched by a mob if he remained in Arkansas, he escaped to Chicago.

Unfortunately, he was captured by local police who agreed with Arkansas authorities to return him to the state. Ida heard about this situation and knew Green would get no fair trial in Arkansas. She, along with attorneys including Ferdinand, negotiated with Illinois authorities to make a deal to prosecute him in Illinois if he did not go across the state line. While on the train heading South to a certain death, Green was taken into custody by a sheriff at the southern tip of Illinois right before crossing into Missouri.

Once back in Chicago, Green was hidden and ultimately escaped to Canada with the assistance of Ida. He returned a few years later, found a night job, and slept during the day at the League until he was able to get on his feet.

A prominent Black lawyer and civil rights activist in post-Reconstruction era Chicago, Ferdinand L. Barnett married Ida B. Wells in 1895 before becoming Illinois' first Black assistant state's attorney in 1896.

Women Belong in the House and Senate and Every Hall of Power

Ida knew that not only did laws need to change, but women needed to get involved in politics. Her husband was an assistant state's attorney. They were both politically and socially engaged in changing things from the inside out. She, and so many who fought for the rights of Black people and all women, paved the way for a succession of trailblazers. In 1917, Jeannette Rankin of Montana became the first woman in either chamber of Congress. In 1968, Shirley Chisholm became the first Black woman to serve in Congress, and she even ran for president in 1972. That same year, Barbara Jordan was the first Black woman to be elected to Congress from the South. The legacy of Ida B. Wells—when it comes to challenging laws, providing support for the most vulnerable citizens, and fighting for political engagement—has lived on for ninety years since her death in 1931.

In 1993, the Illinois representative Carol Moseley Braun became the first Black female senator in the country's history.

As of this writing, almost a quarter of the 116th House of Representatives (101 out of 435) and Senate (26 out of 100) are women. In addition, Nancy Pelosi is the first woman to serve as Speaker of the House. Hundreds of women are mayors of cities and nine women serve as governors. This follows Hillary Clinton, who served as a U.S. senator from New York, and who broke barriers in 2016 by becoming the first woman to be the nominee for a major party in a presidential race.

In 2017, Kamala Harris was the first Black woman to be elected senator for the state of California. She was the second Black woman to run for a major party's presidential nomination, and in August 2020, the year of the centennial of the Nineteenth Amendment, Kamala Harris made history as the first woman of color to be nominated for vice president. The ticket of Joe Biden/Kamala Harris was made possible by the thousands of women who fought for decades for racial and gender equality.

Opposite: The Brooklyn-born Shirley Chisholm was the first African American woman ever elected to the United States House of Representatives. In 1972, she became the first African American candidate for a major party's presidential nomination, and was posthumously awarded the Presidential Medal of Freedom by Barack Obama in 2015.

Below: Nancy Pelosi.

Passing the Torch

Ida B. Wells lived life on her own terms, fighting against an oppressive society that tried its best to keep Black people in a second-class-citizen status. She did not have the right to vote for almost her entire life. She had limited resources compared to the power structure she was fighting. She was a Black woman operating in a white male-dominated society. So, she used the only tool she had—her voice. She spoke up against lynching. She spoke up against segregation. She spoke up against a government that was willing to kill its own soldiers. She organized and marched for the right of women to vote and to have roles in the leadership of the country.

Wherever Ida saw a need to fight for equality, she was on it. In doing this, she endured criticism, financial hardship, terrorism, threats, and enormous loss. Yet she kept on speaking out in order to help the country be all it promised to be. She had a remarkable level of internal fortitude, the courage to speak the truth, and the boldness to challenge systems and social norms that were unjust and limiting. A

Opposite: Carol Moseley Braun. *Left:* Hillary Clinton. *Right:* Barbara Jordan.

woman who was born into slavery went on to take on an entire country—and more. She spoke across the United Kingdom in addition to the United States. She spoke with presidents, governors, mayors, other civil rights activists, women organizers, as well as those who had no home or places to eat. She was uncompromising in her belief of what was right and wrong and believed in herself enough to speak up for what was right.

Despite all her achievements, my great-grandmother did have her low moments. She wrote about how in 1921 while recovering from a health challenge she thought, "All at once the realization came to me that I had nothing to show for all those years of toil and labor." She was human and experienced turmoil and self-doubt at times. But she summed up her overall attitude when she wrote "I could no longer hold my peace, and I feel, yes, I am sure, that if it had to be done over again (provided no one else was the loser save myself) I would do and say the very same again."

We know today that she left an indelible legacy and belief that all people should be treated equally. And the next generation of leaders has her example to follow. The next generation of young women can look at Ida B. Wells and realize that they, too, are capable of tremendous actions. If she could believe in herself enough to not be limited by the circumstances of her birth, so can they. If she could fight for liberty and justice, so can they. Because they, too, are important parts of this world. And their voices matter.

VII.

MONUMENTAL

*Somebody must show that the Afro-American
race is more sinned against than sinning,
and it seems to have fallen upon me to do so.*
—Ida B. Wells

Ida B. Wells Way,
Chicago, Illinois.

Ida's legacy has been preserved and promoted by our family for decades. The multigenerational family efforts to give Ida her due started with my grandmother Alfreda Barnett Duster, who was the youngest of Ida's four children. She edited her mother's autobiography and got it published in 1970. She also donated her papers to her alma mater, the University of Chicago, and her mother's desk to the DuSable Museum of African American History in Chicago.

My father and his siblings started the Ida B. Wells Memorial Foundation in 1988 in order to protect, preserve, and promote their grandmother's legacy. Through the years, they've consulted with authors, filmmakers, museum curators, playwrights, and others who created work about our ancestor.

I became involved in the Foundation in the mid-2000s. We implemented college scholarships at Ida's alma mater, Rust College, to help the next generation of leaders get their educations.

Ida died at the height of the Depression. For the first several decades after she

Left: Rust College.
Below: Alfreda Duster.

Opposite: The Ida B. Wells Homes, 1942, Chicago, Illinois, and dedication poster.

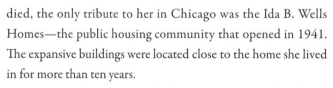

died, the only tribute to her in Chicago was the Ida B. Wells Homes—the public housing community that opened in 1941. The expansive buildings were located close to the home she lived in for more than ten years.

A renewed interest in Ida led to the 1974 national landmark status of her house on 3624 S Dr. Martin Luther King Drive. Two decades later, in 1995, the house was given Chicago landmark status.

Left: Ida B. Wells-Barnett House on S Dr. Martin Luther King Drive, Chicago, Illinois.

Opposite: Ida B. Wells Drive, Chicago, Illinois.

Over twenty-five years will have passed by the time a monument to Ida B. Wells is installed—the first to a Black woman in Chicago. That was after a major downtown street was renamed in 2019 to Ida B. Wells Drive, an honorary street near her house was named Ida B. Wells Way, and a historical marker was placed on that same corner.

These memorials and monuments aren't confined to Chicago. In 1987, a marker was installed on Beale Street in Memphis near the location where her printing press

once existed. The more people learn about my great-grandmother, the more in awe they are. And people want to honor her in ways my family never imagined.

Fitness groups like GirlTrek have created historical walks in Ida's honor. There are social clubs and schools named after her. There was a twenty-five-cent U.S. Heritage stamp created with her image in 1990. A post office in her hometown of Holly Springs was named after her. More recently, a historical marker was placed in the town square.

There are numerous other awards given in Ida's name, as well as tributes such as the 2019 induction into the Mississippi Writers Trail. A room in the Russell Senate Building and a street in Brooklyn were conamed after Ida. And a Baltimore restaurant, Ida B's Table, opened in 2017 and pays homage to her.

Even Google created a doodle for her in 2015, in honor of her 153rd birthday.

Today, more people are carrying on Ida's work through writing, too. The Ida B. Wells Society for Investigative Reporting was cofounded in 2016 by journalists Nikole Hannah-Jones of the *New York Times Magazine*, Topher Sanders of ProPublica,

Ron Nixon of the Associated Press, and Corey Johnson of the *Tampa Bay Times*. The organization provides training and mentorship for journalists of color to compete for positions as investigative journalists who will walk in the footsteps of Ida B. Wells.

The Ida B. Wells-Barnett Museum, created in the 1990s, is located at 200 North Randolph Street in Holly Springs, and so fittingly in the house that was once owned by Spires Boling—the man who enslaved Ida's parents, James and Elizabeth Wells.

My great-grandmother's life was not easy. She endured death threats. She lost friends to lynching. She lost parents through disease. She lost her teaching job when she spoke up against inequality. She lost her printing press when she spoke up against injustice. But through it all, she stayed focused on truth-telling. She believed that her voice was important and her story needed to be heard.

Four generations of my family have worked for more than eight decades to help people remember and honor our foremother, the matriarch of our family—Ida B. Wells-Barnett. We have written about her. Spoken about her. Created books and plays about her. We have worked with politicians and artists. Filmmakers and writers.

Community organizations and students. Schools and municipalities. All to make sure that Ida's story is known.

And today, her bravery, tenacity, and willingness to sacrifice it all is a source of inspiration for current and future generations. She is a giant in our country's history. Little girls today can grow up knowing that they have the right to vote. They have the ability to run for political office. They can reach as high and as far as their talents will take them.

Ida B. Wells did all she could with what she had to work with. She was a teacher, journalist, civil rights activist, suffragist, social worker, wife, and mother. She did not

Below: Ida B. Wells-Barnett Museum, Holly Springs, Mississippi.

Opposite: Ida B. Wells's desk.

let anyone limit her thinking or her dreams. She believed in herself. She believed in the truth. And she left the world better than she found it.

Today, boys and girls across the globe can learn about her strength and focus and believe that they, too, can make a difference in this world. By learning about how someone could be born into slavery, yet go on to have a seismic effect on so many people, they, too, can dare to dream big.

ACKNOWLEDGMENTS

Ida B. the Queen is the result of the incredible vision of Julia Cheiffetz, who saw my great-grandmother Ida B. Wells-Barnett as more than a historic figure. She saw her as someone who is connected to the present and serves as an inspiration for current and future generations.

Between the guidance of Cheiffetz, the skill set and unique perspective of Hannah Giorgis, the gorgeous artwork of Monica Ahanonu, and the photo editing of Nicholas Ciani, the story of Ida's life developed a new vibrancy and relevance that contemporizes her. My agent, Daniel Greenberg, has been an incredible advocate and cheerleader for me during the creation of this book. My hope is that a new generation will be inspired by the extraordinary story of a woman who refused to allow societal restrictions to limit or define her.

I am forever grateful to my brothers, David and Daniel, who have always been supportive of the work involved in the telling of our ancestor's story. Shout-out to my Girlfriends Brunch Club—a group of incredibly smart, witty, down-to-earth friends with whom I can relax, unwind, share laughs, and have fun with. Thank all of you for your friendship and support. To all of my college, high school, and other lifelong friends, you have been my rocks during the ups and downs in this thing called life. To my writing partners Trina Sotira and Bernard C. Turner, thank you for your wisdom and talent. To my aunts, uncles, and cousins who have been with me every step of the way during the decades-long journey of preserving Ida's story, I appreciate all of your encouragement.

This book is dedicated to my mother, Maxine, who always insisted that I embrace my story and my voice; and my father, Donald, who always encouraged

Opposite: Three generations of Ida B. Wells-Barnett descendants—four grandchildren, nine great-grandchildren, and four great-great-grandchildren—and others with Paula J. Giddings (seated, center) at her book launch.

me to take chances in life and believe in myself—you have my forever love and gratitude. Thank you to my grandmother Alfreda Barnett Duster, who always made sure that I knew my history while also insisting that I had my own sense of individual identity. And my great-grandmother Ida B. Wells-Barnett, for being a trailblazer and incredible role model of a Black woman who refused to be quiet, who held her head high, and who challenged systems in order to make this world a better place for everyone.

And to the current and next generations of fierce women! You go! I look forward to seeing how you transform our world.

SOURCES

I. WHO WAS IDA B. WELLS?

1 **the Federal Bureau of Investigation updated its file:** Federal Surveillance of Afro-Americans (1917–1925), Associate Editors Randolph Boehm and R. Dale Grinder, Guide Compiled by Martin Schipper, Reel 10, #116 (file #123754), https://www.fold3.com/image/1433054.

2 **denied the passport:** Becky Little, "See How Women Traveled in 1920," *National Geographic*, August 24, 2018, https://www.nationalgeographic.com/travel/destinations/north-america/united-states/women-equality-day-history-politics-passport.

2 **heinous killing of three Black men:** Linda A. Moore, "125th Anniversary of People's Grocery Lynching Remembered," *Commercial Appeal*, March 9, 2017, https://www.commercialappeal.com/story/news/local/2017/03/09/125th-anniversary-peoples-grocery-lynching-remembered /98607052/.

3 **"crimes" as minor as "being saucy to white people":** Ida B. Wells, *A Red Record: Tabulated Statistics and Alleged Causes of Lynchings in the United States, 1892-1893-1894* (Chicago: self published, 1895).

4 **Ida was one of the founders of the National Association for the Advancement of Colored People (NAACP):** "Nation's Premier Civil Rights Organization," NAACP, https://www.naacp.org/nations-premier-civil-rights-organization.

7 **found the National Association of Colored Women:** "Our History," NACWC, http://nacwc.org/history.

7 **Pulitzer Prize Special Citation:** "Ida B. Wells," The Pulitzer Prizes, https://www.pulitzer.org/winners/ida-b-wells.

III. A VOICE FOR THE PEOPLE

17   **Negro Fellowship League:** Mariame Kaba, "Ida B. Wells-Barnett & the Negro Fellowship League," *Prison Culture* blog, April 18, 2012, https://www.usprisonculture.com/blog/2012/04/18/why-dont-we-know-more-about-the-negro-fellowship-league.

20   **24th Infantry:** Paula J. Giddings, *Ida: A Sword Among Lions: Ida B. Wells and the Campaign Against Lynching* (New York: Amistad Press, 2009), 566–72; Chuck Bauerlein, "When Black Soldiers Fought Back Against Police Brutality 100 Years Ago in Texas," *Philadelphia Inquirer*, August 22, 2017, https://www.inquirer.com/philly/opinion/commentary/police-brutality-race-riot-black-soldiers-hanged-20170822.html.

23   **included Americans of German heritage:** Robert Seigel and Art Silverman, "During World I, U.S. Government Propaganda Erased German Culture," April 7, 2017, in *All Things Considered*, https://www.npr.org/2017/04/07/523044253/during-world-war-i-u-s-government-propaganda-erased-german-culture.

28   **W. E. B. Du Bois:** "NAACP History: W. E. B. Du Bois," NAACP, https://www.naacp.org/naacp-history-w-e-b-dubois.

28   **Tuskegee Airmen:** Zach Giroux, "Rising Above: Tuskegee Airmen, Trailblazers of US Military's First African-American Pilots," *Moultrie News*, February 25, 2020.

30   **A. Philip Randolph:** "A. Philip Randolph," AFL-CIO, https://aflcio.org/about/history/labor-history-people/asa-philip-randolph.

31   **Ella Baker:** "Who Was Ella Baker?," Ella Baker Center for Human Rights, https://ellabakercenter.org/about/who-was-ella-baker.

32   **Adam Clayton Powell Jr.:** "Powell, Adam Clayon, Jr.," Stanford University, The Martin Luther King Jr. Research and Education Institute, https://kinginstitute.stanford.edu/encyclopedia/powell-adam-clayton-jr.

33   **Malcolm X:** Malcolm X, Alex Haley, and Attallah Shabazz, *The Autobiography of Malcolm X* (New York: Ballantine Books, 1992).

34   **significantly excluded from:** Linda O. McMurry, *To Keep the Waters Troubled: The Life of Ida B. Wells* (New York: Oxford University Press, 1998), 304–5.

41   **case was overturned:** "Chesapeake, Ohio & Southwestern Railroad Company v Wells" Tennessee Reports: 85 Cases Argued and Determined in the Supreme Court of Tennessee for the Western Division, Jackson, April Term, 1887, p. 615, Ida B. Papers, [Box 8, Folder 11], Special Collections Research Center, University of Chicago Library https://www.lib.uchicago.edu/ead/pdf/ibwells-0008-011-02.pdf.

44   **extremely rare for a Black woman:** Linda O. McMurry, *To Keep the Waters Troubled: The Life of Ida B. Wells* (New York: Oxford University Press, 1998), 87–90.

IV. HOW IDA BECAME IDA

57–64   **Ida Bell Wells:** Alfreda M. Duster, ed., *Crusade for Justice: The Autobiography of Ida B. Wells*, 2nd ed. (Chicago: University of Chicago Press, 2020).

59   **Dozens of people:** Mackenzie Lanum, "Memphis Riot, 1866," BlackPast, November 20, 2011, https://www.blackpast.org/african-american -history/memphis-riot-1866.

66   **Formerly enslaved women:** Linda O. McMurry, *To Keep the Waters Troubled: The Life of Ida B. Wells* (New York: Oxford University Press, 1998), 25.

66   **Jim Crow law in 1881:** "Jim Crow Laws: Tennessee, 1866–1955," BlackPast, January 03, 2011, https://www.blackpast.org/african-american -history/jim-crow-laws-tennessee-1866-1955/.

V. 400 YEARS OF PROGRESS

68   **Quakers:** History.com Editors, "First American abolition society founded in Philadelphia", https://www.history.com/this-day-in-history/ first-american-abolition-society-founded-in-philadelphia, A&E Television Networks Accessed October 28, 2020.

68   **African Methodist Episcopal Church:** The Editors of Encyclopaedia Britannica, "African Methodist Episcopal Church", March 5, 2020, https://www.britannica.com/topic/African-Methodist-Episcopal -Church, Accessed October 28, 2020.

68   **Frederick Douglass escaped:** Andrew Glass, "Frederick Douglass escapes

from slavery, Sept. 3, 1838," September 3, 2015, https://www.politico. com/story/2015/09/frederick-douglass-escapes-from-slavery-on-sept-3-1838 -213281.

70   **Jim Crow laws:** "Jim Crow Laws: Tennessee, 1866-1955," https://www. blackpast.org/african-american-history/jim-crow-laws-tennessee-1866-1955.

70   **Memphis to Woodstock:** "Ida Wells Case," Digital Public Library of America, http://dp.la/item/8fdc4cecc932be68b7af2180ed2468d8; "The Chesapeake, Ohio and Southwestern Railroad Company vs. Ida B. Wells", Tennessee Virtual Archive, https://teva.contentdm.oclc.org/ digital/collection/p15138coll18/id/176/.

70   **Woodstock to Memphis:** Ibid.

70   **Ida won:** "The Memphis (Tenn.) Appeal Avalanche," December 25, 1884, https:// www.lib.uchicago.edu/ead/pdf/ibwells-0008-011-01.pdf.

70   **lawsuit overturned:** "Chesapeake, Ohio & Southwestern Railroad Company v Wells" Tennessee Reports: 85 Cases Argued and Determined in the Supreme Court of Tennessee for the Western Division, Jackson, April Term, 1887, p. 615, Ida B. Papers, [Box 8, Folder 11], Special Collections Research Center, University of Chicago Library, https:// www.lib.uchicago.edu/ead/pdf/ibwells-0008-011-02.pdf.

71   **Frederick Douglass died:** Steve Hendrix, "Frederick Douglass died Feb. 20, 1895, just hours after his public makeup with Susan B. Anthony" *Washington Post*, February 18, 2019, https://www.washingtonpost.com/ history/2019/02/18/frederick-douglass-died-feb-just-hours-after-his -public-make-up-with-susan-b-anthony/.

71   **Postmaster Frazier B. Baker:** "1898 Postmaster Lynching", https:// postalmuseum.si.edu/exhibition/behind-the-badge-case-histories -assaults-and-murders/1898-postmaster-lynching.

72   **started Negro Fellowship League:** "Ida B. Wells and Sixth-Grace Chicago", https://history.pcusa.org/blog/2016/06/ ida-b-wells-and-sixth-grace-chicago.

72   **formation of NAACP:** "1908 Springfield race riot led to the creation of the NAACP," *State Journal-Register*, August 14, 2018, https://www.sj-r. com/news/20180814/1908-springfield-race-riot-led-to-creation-of-naacp.

72   **Lynching of Will "Frog" James:** Alfreda M. Duster, ed., *Crusade for*

Justice: The Autobiography of Ida B. Wells, 2nd ed. (Chicago: University of Chicago Press, 2020), 263–73; Paula J. Giddings, *Ida: A Sword Among Lions: Ida B. Wells and the Campaign Against Lynching* (New York: Amistad Press, 2008), 482–87.

73 **East St. Louis:** Tabitha Wang, "East St. Louis Race Riot, 1917," Blackpast, June 1, 2008, https://www.blackpast.org/african-american-history/east-st-louis-race-riot-1917.

73 **Houston race riot:** James Jeffrey, "Remembering the Black Soldiers Executed after Houston's 1917 Race Riot," PRI, February 1, 2018, https://www.pri.org/stories/2018-02-01/remembering-black-soldiers-executed-after-houstons-1917-race-riot.

73 **Red Summer:** Olivia B. Waxman, "'It Just Goes On and On': How the Race Riots of 1919's 'Red Summer' Helped Shape a Century of American History," *Time*, July 29, 2019, https://time.com/5636454/what-is-red-summer.

73 **Ida B. Wells Homes:** "March Center Court: Ida B. Wells" Illinois Tech, March 5, 2018, https://www.iit.edu/news/march-center-court-star-ida-b-wells.

74 **Emmett Till:** History.com Editors, "Emmett Till is Murdered", https://www.history.com/this-day-in-history/the-death-of-emmett-till, A&E Television Networks Accessed October 28, 2020.

74 **Rosa Parks's:** Lewis, Femi. "Montgomery Bus Boycott Timeline." ThoughtCo, Aug. 26, 2020, thoughtco.com/montgomery-bus-boycott-timeline-45456.

74 **Voting Rights Act:** https://www.britannica.com/event/Voting-Rights-Act.

74 **Ida B. Wells-Barnett House:** "Illinois: Ida B. Wells-Barnett House Chicago," National Park Service, https://www.nps.gov/places/illinois-ida-b-wellsbarnett-house-chicago.htm.

74 **Tennessee Press Hall of Fame:** "Hall of Fame," Tennessee Press Association, https://tnpress.com/hall-of-fame.

74 **marker on Beale Street:** "Ida B. Wells," Historical Marker Database, https://www.hmdb.org/m.asp?m=9306; "Historical Markers of Shelby County," Shelby County Register of Deeds, https://register.shelby.tn.us/shelby_landmarks/index.php.

74 **National Women's Hall of Fame:** "Ida B. Wells-Barnett," National Women's Hall of Fame, https://www.womenofthehall.org/inductee/ida-b-wellsbarnett.

75 **postage stamp:** "Ida B. Wells," National Postal Museum, https://postalmuseum.si.edu/exhibition/the-black-experience-prominent-journalists/ida-b-wells.

75 **Historical marker installed for People's Grocery:** "People's Grocery Historical Marker," Lynching Sites Project Memphis, https://lynchingsitesmem.org/archives/peoples-grocery-historical-marker; Lee Eric Smith, "Historic Marker Unveiled at Gravesite of 'People's Grocery Lynchings,'" *New Tri-State Defender*, March 29, 2019, https://tri-statedefender.com/historic-marker-unveiled-at-gravesite-of-peoples-grocery-lynchings/03/29.

75 **Ida B. Wells-Barnett House designated:** "Ida B. Wells-Barnett House," City of Chicago, https://webapps1.chicago.gov/landmarksweb/web/landmarkdetails.htm?lanId=1453.

75 **Ida B. Wells-Barnett Museum:** Ida B. Wells-Barnett Museum website http://idabwellsmuseum.org.

75 **Ida B. Wells Homes in Chicago started being demolished:** Jake Bittle, Srishti Kapur, and Jasmine Mithani, "Redeveloping the State Street Corridor," *South Side Weekly*, January 31, 2017, https://southsideweekly.com/chicago-unfulfilled-promise-rebuild-public-housing.

75 **United States Senate issued a resolution:** "Senate Apologizes for Inaction on Lynchings," NBC News, June 13, 2005, https://www.nbcnews.com/id/wbna8206697#.X0Kv56eSnIU.

75 **S Res 39:** "S.Res. 39 (109th): Lynching Victims Senate Apology Resolution," GovTrack, https://www.govtrack.us/congress/bills/109/sres39/text.

76 **Russell Building**—invitation to Ida B. Wells's descendants from United States Senate Committee on Small Business and Entrepreneurship Chair Mary L. Landrieu; April 2010.

76 **Chicago Literary Hall of Fame:** "Ida B. Wells," Chicago Literary Hall of Fame, https://chicagoliteraryhof.org/inductees/profile/ida-b.-wells.

76 **Ida B. Wells Society:** "Our Creation Story," The Ida B. Wells Society, https://idabwellssociety.org/about/our-creation-story.

76   **National Museum of African American History and Culture:** "About the Museum," National Museum of African American History and Culture, https://nmaahc.si.edu/about/museum.

76   *New York Times* **obituary:** Caitlin Dickerson, "Ida B. Wells, Who Took on Racism in the Deep South with Powerful Reporting on Lynchings," *New York Times*, 2018, https://www.nytimes.com/interactive/2018/obituaries/overlooked-ida-b-wells.html.

76   *New York Times The Daily* **podcast:** Michael Barbaro, "Listen to 'The Daily': Women We Overlooked," *New York Times*, March 16, 2018, https://www.nytimes.com/2018/03/16/podcasts/the-daily/ida-b-wells-overlooked-obituaries.html.

76   **Legacy Museum:** The Legacy Museum: From Enslavement to Mass Incarceration website, https://museumandmemorial.eji.org/museum.

76   **Congress Parkway in Chicago renamed Ida B. Wells Drive:** Gregory Pratt and John Byrne, "Ida B. Wells Gets Her Street—City Council Approves Renaming Congress in Her Honor," *Chicago Tribune*, July 25, 2018, https://www.chicagotribune.com/politics/ct-met-rahm-emanual-ida-b-wells-street-20180725-story.html.

76   **Ida B. Wells Drive street sign unveiling ceremony:** Mary Mitchell, "Ida B. Wells Finally Gets a Top Honor with Street Name," *Chicago Sun Times*, February 11, 2019, https://chicago.suntimes.com/2019/2/11/18328682/ida-b-wells-finally-gets-a-top-honor-with-street-name.

76   **Senate antilynching bill:** Justice for Victims of Lynching Act of 2019, S. 488, 116th Cong., (2019), https://www.congress.gov/bill/116th-congress/senate-bill/488.

76   **House antilynching bill:** Emmett Till Antilynching Act, H.R. 35, 116th Cong., (2020), https://www.congress.gov/bill/116th-congress/house-bill/35/text/ih.

76   **Rand Paul:** David Smith, "Rand Paul Stalls Bill That Would Make Lynching a Federal Hate Crime," *Guardian*, June 11, 2020, https://www.theguardian.com/us-news/2020/jun/11/rand-paul-lynching-hate-crime-bill-limbo.

77   **Ida B. Wells Way and historical marker:** Megann Horstead, "Plaque and

Honorary Street Sign Unveiled in Memory of Ida B. Wells," *Chicago Defender*, July 25, 2019, https://chicagodefender.com/plaque-and-honorary -street-sign-unveiled-in-memory-of-ida-b-wells.

77   **Mississippi Writers Trail:** Reggi Marion, "Literary Lawn Party: Mississippi Book Festival Held in Jackson," WLBT, August 17, 2019, https://www.wlbt.com/2019/08/17/literary-lawn-party-mississippi -book-festival-held-jackson.

77   **Pulitzer Prize Special Citation:** "Ida B. Wells," The Pulitzer Prizes, / ida-b-wells. https://www.pulitzer.org.

77   **Edward Carmack:** "Nashville Protesters Set Fires, Topple Controversial Statue," Associated Press, May 30, 2020, https://apnews.com/ 2e7f5b2a93025df5b4343fc14184842c.

77   **Ida B. Wells Plaza:** Brinley Hineman and Natalie Allison, "Protesters Plan to Camp Out in Front of Capitol, Claiming Area as Autonomous Zone," *Tennessean*, June 12, 2020, https://www.tennessean.com/story/news/ politics/2020/06/12/nashville-capitol-hill-autonomous-zone-not -tolerated-gov-bill-lee/3176168001/.

VI. A POWERFUL LEGACY

78   **They had destroyed my paper:** Alfreda M. Duster, ed., *Crusade for Justice: The Autobiography of Ida B. Wells*, 2nd ed. (Chicago: University of Chicago Press, 2020).

78   **the ideal woman was seen:** Linda O. McMurry, *To Keep the Waters Troubled: A Life of Ida B. Wells* (New York: Oxford University Press, 2000).

80   **Recy Taylor:** "Recy Taylor, Rosa Parks, and the Struggle for Racial Justice," National Museum of African American History and Culture blog, https:// nmaahc.si.edu/blog-post/recy-taylor-rosa-parks-and-struggle-racial-justice; The Rape of Recy Taylor website, https://www.therapeofrecytaylor.com/ the-film.

82   **Daniel Holtzclaw:** Madeline Holcombe and Eliott C. McLaughlin, "Oklahoma Ex-officer Convicted of Raping Multiple Women is Denied an Appeal," CNN, August 2, 2019; https://www.cnn.com/2019/08/02/ us/holtzclaw-appeal-denied/index.html.

83   **Sarah Baartman:** "Saartjie (Sarah) Baartman's Story," Saartjie Baartman

Centre for Women and Children, http://www.saartjiebaartmancentre.org.za/about-us/saartjie-baartmans-story.

89   **the Black Lives Matter movement:** Black Lives Matter website, https://blacklivesmatter.com/about; Jamiles Lartey, "Obama on Black Lives Matter: They Are 'Much Better Organizers Than I Was,'" *Guardian*, February 18, 2016, https://www.theguardian.com/us-news/2016/feb/18/.black-lives-matter-meet-president-obama-white-house-justice-system.

90   **Reconstruction:** Adam Serwer, "Civility Is Overrated," *Atlantic*, December 2019, https://www.theatlantic.com/magazine/archive/2019/12/adam-serwer-civility/600784.

91   **Sister Souljah:** David Mills, "Sister Souljah's Call to Arms," *Washington Post*, May 13, 1992, https://www.washingtonpost.com/archive/lifestyle/1992/05/13/sister-souljahs-call-to-arms/643d5634-e622-43ad-ba7d-811f8f5bfe5d.

94   **Bree Newsome:** Lottie Joiner, "Bree Newsome Reflects on Taking Down South Carolina's Confederate Flag 2 Years Ago," Vox, June 27, 2017, https://www.vox.com/identities/2017/6/27/15880052/bree-newsome-south-carolinas-confederate-flag.

94   **Dylann Roof:** Bim Adewunmi, "Dylann Roof Is an American Problem," *BuzzFeed News*, January 14, 2017, https://www.buzzfeednews.com/article/bimadewunmi/dylann-roof-is-an-american-problem.

97   **Colin Kaepernick:** John Branch, "The Awakening of Colin Kaepernick," *New York Times*, September 7, 2017, https://www.nytimes.com/2017/09/07/sports/colin-kaepernick-nfl-protests.html.

97   **End Racism:** "NFL to Feature Social Justice Messages in End Zones This Season," Associated Press, September 1, 2020, https://www.si.com/nfl/2020/09/01/nfl-end-zone-social-justice-slogans-end-racism.

98   **Muhammad Ali:** Krishnadev Calamur, "Muhammad Ali and Vietnam," *Atlantic*, June 4, 2016, https://www.theatlantic.com/news/archive/2016/06/muhammad-ali-vietnam/485717.

98   **gold medalist Tommie Smith and the bronze medalist John Carlos:** Gary Younge, "The Man Who Raised a Black Power Salute at the 1968 Olympic Games," *Guardian*, March 30, 2012, https://www.theguardian.com/world/2012/mar/30/black-power-salute-1968-olympics.

102   **Antilynching law:** Amanda Shendruk, "The US has failed to pass anti-lynching laws 240 times. This is all of them," Quartz, July 10, 2018, https://qz.com/1322702/the-us-has-tried-to-pass-anti-lynching-laws -240-times-and-failed-every-single-time/.

113   **John H. Johnson:** Kelly Connelly, "Arkansas Holiday to Celebrate the Life of Pioneering Black Publisher," Public Radio from UA Little Rock, October 31, 2019, https://www.ualrpublicradio.org/post/arkansas-holiday -celebrate-life-pioneering-black-publisher.

114   **1619 Project:** *New York Times* magazine staff, "The 1619 Project," *New York Times Magazine*, August 14, 2019, https://www.nytimes.com/ interactive/2019/08/14/magazine/1619-america-slavery.html.

115   **Central Park Five:** Aisha Harris, "The Central Park Five: 'We Were Just Baby Boys,'" *New York Times*, May 30, 2019, https://www.nytimes.com/ 2019/05/30/arts/television/when-they-see-us.html.

118   **Maxine Waters:** Mekita Rivas, "Maxine Waters Was the First to Call for Impeachment. Here's What She's Calling for Next," Shondaland, February 10, 2020, https://www.shondaland.com/act/news-politics/ a30814592/maxine-waters-impeachment.

121   **Lucy McBath:** Jelani Cobb, "The Crucial Significance of Lucy McBath's Win in Georgia's Sixth Congressional District," *New Yorker*, November 17, 2018, https://www.newyorker.com/news/daily-comment/the-crucial -significance-of-lucy-mcbaths-win-in-georgias-sixth-congressional-district.

124   **Abrams refused:** Laura Bassett, "Stacey Abrams Acknowledges Loss in Governor's Race," *HuffPost*, November 16, 2018, https://www.huffpost. com/entry/stacey-abrams-acknowledges-loss-in-georgia-gover- nors-race_n_5bef4370e4b0b84243e25ece; Fair Fight "Meet Our Founder" https://fairfight.com/about-stacey-abrams/.

124   **Black Lives Matter movement:** Ellen Kershner, "What Is The Black Lives Matter Movement?", World Atlas, June 4, 2020, https://www .worldatlas.com/articles/what-is-the-black-lives-matter-movement.html.

124   **Black Youth Project 100:** "About Us" http://blackyouthproject.com/ about-us/.

124   **Movement for Black Lives:** "Vision for Black Lives" https://m4bl.org/ policy-platforms/.

124   **During the 1970s:** Winifred Breines, "Struggling to Connect: White and Black Feminism in the Movement Years," *Contexts*. 2007; 6(1):18-24. doi :10.1525/ctx.2007.6.1.18 https://journals.sagepub.com/doi/abs/10.1525/ctx.2007.6.1.18#articleCitationDownloadContainer.

125   **Featured a suffrage float:** Ryan Carter, "This Rose Parade float celebrates 100 years since women won the right to vote" *Pasadena Star News*, December 30, 2019, https://www.pasadenastarnews.com/2019/12/30/this-rose-parade-float-celebrates-100-years-since-women-won-the-right-to-vote/.

126   **penniless Black man:** Alfreda M. Duster, ed., *Crusade for Justice: The Autobiography of Ida B. Wells*, 2nd ed. (Chicago: University of Chicago Press, 2020), 263–73; Paula J. Giddings, *Ida: A Sword Among Lions: Ida B. Wells and the Campaign Against Lynching* (New York: Amistad Press, 2008), 482–87.

127   **NAACP's Legal Defense and Educational Fund:** "About Us" https://www.naacpldf.org/about-us.

127   **First Defense Legal Aid:** "About Us" https://www.first-defense.org/about/.

127   **opened the Negro Fellowship League:** Alfreda M. Duster, ed., *Crusade for Justice: The Autobiography of Ida B. Wells*, 2nd ed. (Chicago: University of Chicago Press, 2020), 259.

127   **Ferdinand was assistant state's attorney:** F. L Barnett Candidate For Alderman of the 2nd, *The Broad Ax* (Salt Lake City, Utah) February 24, 1917, page 4 https://www.newspapers.com/clip/6653894/the-broad-ax/.

129   **Steve Green:** Alfreda M. Duster, ed., *Crusade for Justice: The Autobiography of Ida B. Wells*, 2nd ed. (Chicago: University of Chicago Press, 2020), 286–87; Paula J. Giddings, *Ida: A Sword Among Lions: Ida B. Wells and the Campaign Against Lynching* (New York: Amistad Press, 2008), 494–97.

130   **a quarter of the 116th House:** Drew DeSilver, "A record number of women will be serving in the new Congress," Pew Research Center, December 18, 2018, https://www.pewresearch.org/fact-tank/2018/12/18/record-number-women-in-congress/.

VII. MONUMENTAL

136   **Ida B. Wells Memorial Foundation:** "Home," www.ibwfoundation.org.

139   **public housing community:** "March Center Court: Ida B. Wells," Illinois

Tech, March 5, 2018, https://www.iit.edu/news/march-center-court-star
-ida-b-wells.

139   **1974 national landmark:** "Ida B. Wells-Barnett House," http://
landmarkhunter.com/148539-ida-wells-barnett-house/.

139   **Chicago landmark status:** "Ida B. Wells-Barnett House," City of Chicago,
https://webapps1.chicago.gov/landmarksweb/web/ landmarkdetails
.htm?lanId=1453; "Chicago Landmarks"—Ida B. Wells-Barnett House,
https://web.archive.org/web/20070607163021/http://www.ci.chi.il.us/
Landmarks/I/IdaBWells.html.

141   **monument to Ida B. Wells:** "The Monument," http://idabwellsmonu-
ment.org/newsite4/the-monument/; Liz Dwyer, "There Are No Ida B.
Wells Monuments in America. Her Great-Granddaughter Is Out to
Change That," *Shondaland*, July 16, 2018, https://www.shondaland.
com/inspire/a22145974/there-no-ida-b-wells-monument-in-america
-her-great-granddaughter-is-out-to-change-that/.

141   **Ida B. Wells Drive:** Mary Mitchell, "Ida B. Wells Finally Gets a Top
Honor with Street Name," *Chicago Sun Times*, February 11, 2019, https://
chicago.suntimes.com/2019/2/11/18328682/ ida-b-wells-finally-gets
-a-top-honor-with-street-name.

141   **Ida. B. Wells Way:** Megann Horstead, "Plaque and Honorary Street Sign
Unveiled in Memory of Ida B. Wells," *Chicago Defender*, July 25, 2019,
https://chicagodefender.com/plaque-and-honorary-street-sign-unveiled
-in-memory-of-ida-b-wells.

141   **Beale Street in Memphis:** "Ida B. Wells," Historical Marker Database,
https://www.hmdb.org/m.asp?m=9306.

142   **like GirlTrek:** "Our Mission" https://www.girltrek.org/our_mission.

142   **Heritage stamp:** "Ida B. Wells," National Postal Museum, https://
postalmuseum.si.edu/exhibition/the-black-experience-prominent
-journalists/ida-b-wells.

142   **Mississippi Writers Trail:** Reggi Marion, "Literary Lawn Party:
Mississippi Book Festival Held in Jackson," WLBT, August 17, 2019,
https://www.wlbt.com/2019/08/17/literary-lawn-party-mississippi-book
-festival-held-jackson.

142   **Russell Senate Building:** invitation to Ida B. Wells's descendants from

United States Senate Committee on Small Business and Entrepreneurship Chair Mary L. Landrieu; April 2010.

142   **street in Brooklyn:** Karen Juanita Carrillo, "Ida B. Wells Place is designated in Downtown Brooklyn," *New York Amsterdam News*, March 19, 2020, http://amsterdamnews.com/news/2020/mar/19/ida-b-wells-place -designated-downtown-brooklyn/.

142   **Ida B's Table:** Sarah Meehan, "Ida B's Table Opening Downtown This Summer," *Baltimore Sun*, May 25, 2017, https://www.baltimoresun. com/food-drink/bs-fo-ida-bs-table-20170525-story.html; www. idabstable.com/about.

142   **Ida B. Wells Society:** "Our Creation Story," The Ida B. Wells Society, https://idabwellssociety.org/about/our-creation-story.

143   **Ida B. Wells-Barnett Museum:** "About," http://idabwellsmuseum.org/ about/.

IMAGE CREDITS

INDEX